ROOKIE COACHES FOOTBALL GUIDE

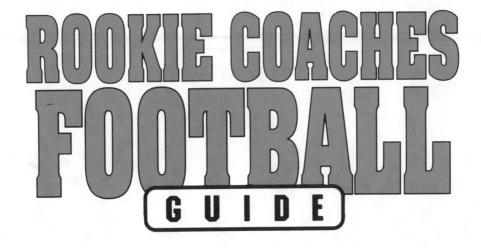

American Coaching Effectiveness Program

endorsed by
Pop Warner Football

Human Kinetics Publishers

Library of Congress Cataloging-in-Publication Data

Rookie coaches football guide / American Coaching Effectiveness
    Program.
        p.   cm.
    ISBN 0-87322-389-6
        1. Youth league football--Coaching.   I. American Coaching
    Effectiveness Program.
    GV956.6.R66   1993
    796.332'07'7--dc20   92-22875
                                                                CIP

ISBN: 0-87322-389-6

Developmental Editor: Ted Miller
Managing Editor: Jan Colarusso Seeley
Football Consultant: Mel Olson, Brigham Young University
Assistant Editor: Laura Bofinger
Copyeditor: Barbara Walsh
Proofreader: Tom Rice
Production Director: Ernie Noa
Typesetter: Julie Overholt
Text Design: Keith Blomberg
Text Layout: Kimberlie Henris
Cover Design: Jack Davis
Cover Photo: John Kilroy/Photo Concepts
Interior Art: Tim Stiles and Tim Offenstein
Printer: United Graphics

Human Kinetics books are available at special discounts for bulk purchase for sales promotions, premiums, fund-raising, or educational use. Special editions or book excerpts can also be created to specification. For details, contact the Special Sales Manager at Human Kinetics.

Printed in the United States of America

10 9 8 7 6 5 4 3 2 1

Human Kinetics Publishers
Box 5076, Champaign, IL 61825-5076
1-800-747-4457

Canada Office:
P.O. Box 2503, Windsor, ON N8Y 4S2
1-800-465-7301 (in Canada only)

Europe Office:
Human Kinetics Publishers (Europe) Ltd.
P.O. Box IW14
Leeds LS16 6TR
England
0532-781708

Australia Office:
Human Kinetics Publishers
P.O. Box 80
Kingswood 5062
South Australia
374-0433

Contents

A Message From Pop Warner Football

We are extremely supportive of efforts to educate and certify youth football coaches. For one reason, volunteers like you will learn the important principles of coaching and how to apply them to your sport. But another reason—at least as important—is that this instruction can make you even more sensitive to the needs of your players.

By treating your athletes in a positive, understanding way, you'll develop their enthusiasm for football, which will promote future participation in this great sport. At the same time, you'll help change the negative stereotype of the untrained, insensitive youth football coach to a more accurate and positive perception.

Pop Warner Football supports the Athletes First, Winning Second philosophy of the American Coaching Effectiveness Program. And we strongly encourage you to use this *Rookie Coaches Football Guide* as a resource for teaching your players the game while making their experience as safe and fun as possible.

Welcome to Coaching!

Coaching young people is an exciting way to be involved in sport. But it isn't easy. Some coaches are overwhelmed by the responsibilities involved in helping athletes through their early sport experiences. And that's not surprising, because coaching youngsters requires more than bringing the footballs and equipment to the field and letting them play. It involves preparing them physically and mentally to compete effectively, fairly, and safely in their sport and providing them a positive role model.

This book will help you meet the challenges *and* experience the many rewards of coaching young athletes. We call it the *Rookie Coaches Football Guide* because it is intended for adults with little or no formal preparation in coaching football. In this book you'll learn how to apply general coaching principles and teach football rules, skills, and strategies successfully to kids.

The American Coaching Effectiveness Program (ACEP) thanks Dr. Mel Olson, a former college football player and assistant coach at Brigham Young University and now a coaching educator and athlete advisor at the same school, for contributing his football coaching expertise to the book. We also thank Pop Warner Football for reviewing and endorsing the book. Combining this great understanding of youth football with ACEP's expertise in important coaching principles, this *Rookie Coaches Guide* is the best playbook any youth football coach could use to start off the season.

This book also serves as a text for ACEP's Rookie Coaches Course. If you would like more information about this course or ACEP, please contact us at

ACEP
Box 5076
Champaign, IL 61825-5076
1-800-747-4457

Good Coaching!

Who, Me . . . a Coach?

If you're like most youth league coaches, you were recruited from the ranks of concerned parents, sport enthusiasts, or community volunteers. And, like many rookie *and* veteran coaches, you probably have had little formal instruction on how to coach. But when the call went out for coaches to assist with the local youth football program, you answered because you like children, enjoy football, are community-minded, and perhaps are interested in starting a coaching career.

I Want to Help, But . . .

Your initial coaching assignment may be difficult. Like many volunteers, you may not know everything there is to know about football, nor about how to work with children aged 7 through 14. Relax, this *Rookie Coaches Football Guide* will help you learn the basics for coaching football effectively. In the coming pages you will find the answers to such common questions as these:

- What tools do I need to be a good coach?
- How can I best communicate with my players?
- How do I go about teaching sport skills?
- What can I do to promote safety?
- What actions do I take when someone is injured?
- What are the basic rules, skills, and strategies of football?
- What practice drills will improve my players' football skills?

Before answering these questions, let's take a look at what's involved in being a coach.

Am I a Parent or a Coach?

Many coaches are parents, but the two roles should not be confused. As a parent you are responsible only to yourself and your child; as a coach you are responsible to the organization, all the players on the team (including your child), and their parents.

Because of these additional responsibilities, your behavior on the football field will be different than it is at home, and your son may not understand why. Take these steps to avoid problems when coaching your child:

- Ask your child if he wants you to coach the team.
- Explain why you wish to be involved with the team.
- Discuss with your child your new responsibilities and how they will affect your relationship when coaching.
- Limit your "coach" behavior to those times when you are in a coaching role.
- Avoid parenting during practice or game situations to keep your role clear in your child's mind.
- Reaffirm your love for your child irrespective of his performance on the football field.

What Are My Responsibilities as a Coach?

A coach assumes the responsibility of doing everything possible to ensure that the youngsters on his team will have an enjoyable and safe sporting experience while they learn sport skills. If you're ever in doubt about your approach, remind yourself that "fun and fundamentals" are most important.

Provide an Enjoyable Experience

Football should be fun. Even if nothing else is accomplished, make certain your players have fun. Take the fun out of football and you'll take the kids out of football.

Children enter sport for a number of reasons (e.g., to meet and play with other children, to develop physically, to learn skills), but their major objective is to have fun. Help them satisfy this goal by injecting humor and variety into your practices. Also, make games nonthreatening, festive experiences for your players. Such an approach will increase their desire to participate in the future, which should be the primary goal of youth sport.

Unit 2 will help you learn how to satisfy your players' yearning for fun and keep winning in perspective. And Unit 3 will describe how to communicate this perspective effectively to them.

Provide a Safe Experience

If one thing keeps kids out of football, it's the risk of injury. Children will not participate—and will not be allowed to participate by their parents—unless responsible safety measures are taken by the league and by you, the coach.

You are responsible for planning and teaching activities in such a way that the progression between activities minimizes risks (see Units 4 and 5). You also must ensure that the facility at which your team practices and plays, and the equipment team members use, are free of hazards. Finally, you need to protect yourself from any legal liability issues that might arise from your involvement as a coach. Unit 5 will help you take the appropriate precautions.

Teach Basic Football Skills

In becoming a coach, you take on the role of educator. You must teach your players the fundamental skills and strategies necessary for success in football. That means that you need to "go to school." If you don't know the basics of football now, you can learn them by reading the second half of this manual. And even if you know football as a player, do you know how to teach it? This book will help you get started.

Many more valuable football books are available, including those offered by Human Kinetics Publishers. See the books listed in the back of this book and call 1-800-747-4457 to ask ACEP for more information.

You'll also find that you are better able to teach the football skills and strategies you do know if you plan your practices. Unit 4 of this manual provides guidelines for effective practice planning.

Who Can Help?

Veteran coaches in your league are an especially good source of information and assistance. So are high school and college coaches. These coaches have experienced the same emotions and concerns you are facing; their advice and feedback can be invaluable as you work through your first few seasons of coaching.

You can also learn a great deal by observing local football coaches in practices and games. You might even ask a few of the coaches you respect most to lend a hand with a couple of your practices.

You can get additional help by attending football clinics, reading football publications, and studying instructional videos. Contact ACEP or write or call Pop Warner at

Pop Warner Football
920 Town Center Drive
Suite I-25
Langhorne, PA 19047
(215) 752-2691

Coaching football is a rewarding experience. And, just as you want your players to learn and practice to be the best they can be, learn all you can about coaching so you can be the best football coach you can be.

UNIT 2

What Tools Do I Need to Coach?

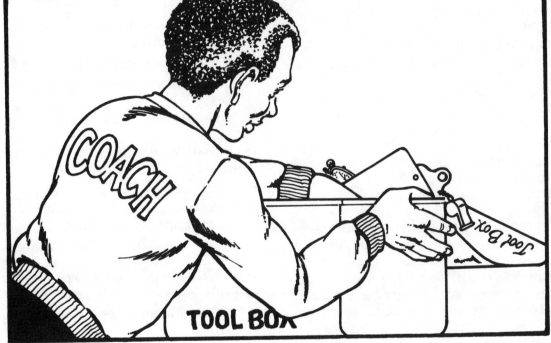

Have you acquired the traditional coaching tools—things like footballs, a whistle, a clipboard, and a first aid kit? They'll help you coach, but to be a successful coach you'll need five other *tools* that cannot be bought. These tools are available only through self-examination and hard work, but they're easy to remember with the acronym COACH:

C—Comprehension

O—Outlook

A—Affection

C—Character

H—Humor

Comprehension

Comprehension of the rules, skills, and tactics of football is required. It is essential that you understand the basic elements of the sport. To assist you in learning about the game, the second half of this guide describes general game procedures as well as specific football techniques and strategies. In the football-specific section of this guide, you'll also find a variety of drills to use in developing young players' football skills. And, perhaps most importantly, you'll learn how to use your knowledge of the game most effectively when teaching your football team.

To improve your comprehension of football, take the following steps:

- Read the sport-specific section of this book.
- Consider reading other coaching books, including those available from ACEP (see p. 76).
- Contact Pop Warner Football (see p. 3).
- Attend football coaches' clinics.
- Talk with other, more experienced football coaches.
- Observe local college, high school, and youth football games.
- Study football games on television.

In addition to having football knowledge, you must implement proper training and safety methods so your players can participate with less risk of injury. Even then, sport injuries will occur. And, more often than not, you'll be the first person responding to your players' injuries. Therefore, make sure you understand the basic emergency care procedures described in Unit 5. Also read in that unit how to handle more serious sport injury situations.

Outlook

This coaching tool refers to your perspective and goals—what you are seeking as a coach. The most common coaching objectives are (a) to have fun, (b) to help players develop their physical, mental, and social skills, and (c) to win. Thus, *outlook* involves the priorities you set, your planning, and your vision for the future.

To work successfully with children in a sport setting, you must have your priorities in order. In just what order do you rank the importance of fun, development, and winning?

Answer the following questions to examine your objectives.

Of which situation would you be most proud?
a. Knowing that each participant enjoyed playing football.
b. Seeing that all players improved their football skills.
c. Winning the league championship.

Which statement best reflects your thoughts about sport?
a. If it isn't fun, don't do it.
b. Everyone should learn something every day.
c. Football isn't fun if you don't win.

How would you like your players to remember you?
a. As a coach who was fun to play for.
b. As a coach who helped players develop good fundamental skills.
c. As a coach who had a winning record.

Which would you most like to hear a parent of a child on your team say?
a. Billy really had a good time playing football this year.
b. Brian learned some important lessons playing football this year.
c. Mike played on the first-place football team this year.

Which of the following would be the most rewarding moment of your season?
a. Having your team not want to stop playing even after practice is over.
b. Seeing your players learn how to get off the ball quickly, as a unit, when the ball is snapped.
c. Winning a game on a play you called.

Look over your answers. If you most often selected "a" responses, then having fun is more important to you. A majority of "b" answers suggests that skill development is what attracts you to coaching. And if "c" was your most frequent response, winning is tops on your list of coaching priorities.

Most coaches say fun and development are more important, but when actually coaching, some coaches emphasize—indeed overemphasize— winning. You too will face situations that challenge you to keep winning in its proper perspective. During such moments you may have to choose between emphasizing your players' development and winning. If your priorities are in order, your players' well-being will take precedence over your team's win-loss record every time.

Take the following actions to better define your outlook:

- Determine your priorities for the season.
- Prepare for situations that challenge your priorities.
- Set goals for yourself and your players that are consistent with those priorities.
- Plan how you and your players can best attain those goals.
- Review your goals frequently to be sure that you are staying on track.

It is particularly important for coaches to permit all young athletes to participate. Each youngster should have an opportunity to develop skills and have fun—even if it means sacrificing a win or two during the season. After all, wouldn't you prefer losing a couple of games to losing a couple of players' interest in football?

Remember that the challenge and joy of sport is experienced through *striving to win*, not through winning itself. Players who aren't allowed off the bench are denied the opportunity to strive to win. And herein lies the irony: A coach who allows all of his or her players to participate and develop skills will, in the end, come out on top.

ACEP has a motto that will help you keep your outlook in the best interest of the kids on your team. It summarizes in four words all you need to remember when establishing your coaching priorities:

Athletes First, Winning Second

This motto recognizes that striving to win is an important, even vital part of sport. But it emphatically states that no efforts in striving to win should be made at the expense of athletes' well-being, development, and enjoyment.

Affection

This is another vital *tool* you will want to have in your coaching kit: a genuine concern for the young people you coach. *Affection* involves having a love for children, a desire to share with them your love and knowledge of football, and the patience and understanding that allows each child playing for you to grow through his participation.

Successful coaches have a real concern for the health and welfare of their players. They care that each child on the team has an enjoyable and successful experience. They have a strong desire to work with children and be involved in their growth. And they have the patience to work with those who are slower to learn or less capable of performing. If you have such qualities or are willing to work hard to develop them, then you have the affection necessary to coach young athletes.

There are many ways to demonstrate your affection and patience, including the following:

- Make an effort to get to know each player on your team.
- Treat each player as an individual.
- Empathize with players trying to learn new and difficult football skills.
- Treat players as you would like to be treated under similar circumstances.
- Be in control of your emotions.
- Show your enthusiasm for being involved with your team.
- Keep an upbeat and positive tone in all of your communications.

Character

Youngsters learn by listening to what adults say. But they learn even more by watching the behaviors of certain important individuals. As a coach, you are likely to be a significant figure in the lives of your players. Will you be a good role model?

Having good *character* means modeling appropriate behaviors for sport and life. That means more than just saying the right things. What you say and what you do must match. There is no place in coaching for the "Do as I say, not as I do" philosophy. Be in control of yourself before, during, and after all games and practices. And don't be afraid to admit that you were wrong. No one is perfect!

Consider the following steps to being a good role model:

- Take stock of your strengths and weaknesses.
- Build on your strengths.
- Set goals for yourself to improve upon those areas you would not like to see mimicked.
- If you slip up, apologize to your team and to yourself. You'll do better next time.

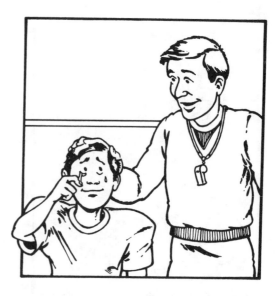

Humor

Humor is often overlooked as a coaching tool. For our purposes it means having the ability to laugh *at* yourself and *with* your players during practices and games.

Nothing helps balance the tone of a serious, skill-learning session like a chuckle or two. And a sense of humor puts in perspective the many mistakes your young players will make. So don't get upset over each miscue or respond negatively to erring players. Allow your players and yourself to enjoy the "ups" and don't dwell on the "downs."

Here are some tips for injecting humor into your practices:

- Make practices fun by including a variety of activities.
- Keep all players involved in drills and scrimmages.
- Consider laughter by your players a sign of enjoyment, not a lack of discipline.
- Smile!

Where Do You Stand?

To take stock of your "coaching tool kit," rank yourself on each of the three questions concerning the five coaching tools. Simply circle the number that best describes your *present* status on each item.

Not at all		Somewhat		Very much so
1	2	3	4	5

Comprehension

1.	Could you explain the rules of football to players' parents without studying for a long time?	1 2 3 4 5
2.	Do you know how to organize and conduct safe football practices?	1 2 3 4 5
3.	Do you know how to provide first aid for most common, minor sport injuries?	1 2 3 4 5

Comprehension Score: _____

Outlook

4.	Do you have winning in its proper perspective when you coach?	1 2 3 4 5
5.	Do you plan for every meeting, practice, and game?	1 2 3 4 5
6.	Do you have a vision of what you want your players to be able to do by the end of the season?	1 2 3 4 5

Outlook Score: _____

Affection

7.	Do you enjoy working with children?	1 2 3 4 5
8.	Are you patient with youngsters learning new skills?	1 2 3 4 5
9.	Are you able to show your players that you care about them on and off the field?	1 2 3 4 5

Affection Score: _____

Character

10.	Are your words and behaviors consistent with each other?	1 2 3 4 5
11.	Are you a good model for your players?	1 2 3 4 5
12.	Do you keep negative emotions under control before, during, and after games?	1 2 3 4 5

Character Score: _____

(Cont.)

Continued

Not at all		Somewhat		Very much so
1	2	3	4	5

Humor

13. Do you usually smile at your players?   1 2 3 4 5
14. Are your practices fun?   1 2 3 4 5
15. Are you able to laugh at your mistakes?   1 2 3 4 5

Humor Score: _____

If you scored 9 or less on any of the coaching tools, be sure to reread those sections carefully. And even if you scored 15 on each tool, don't be complacent. Keep learning! Then you'll be well equipped with the tools you need to coach young athletes.

UNIT 3

How Should I Communicate With My Players?

Now you know the tools needed to COACH; Comprehension, Outlook, Affection, Character, and Humor are essential for effective coaching. Without them, you'd have a difficult time getting started. But none of these tools will work unless you know how to use them with your athletes—that requires skillful communication. This unit examines what communication is and how you can become a more effective communicator-coach.

What's Involved in Communication?

Coaches often believe that communication involves only instructing players to run

11

certain plays or drills, but these verbal commands are a very small part of the communication process. More than half of what is communicated in a message is nonverbal. So remember when you are coaching, "actions speak louder than words."

Communication in its simplest form is like a quarterback and a receiver. It involves two people: one to pass the message (verbally, through facial expression, and via body language) and the other to receive it. Of course, a receiver who fails to pay attention or judge the message correctly will not catch it.

How Can I Send More Effective Messages?

Young athletes often have little understanding of the rules and skills of football, and probably even have less confidence in playing it. So they need you to provide them accurate, understandable, and supportive messages.

Verbal Messages

"Sticks and stones may break my bones, but words will never hurt me" isn't true. Spoken words can have a strong and long-lasting effect. And coaches' words are particularly influential, because youngsters place great importance on what coaches say. Therefore,

whether you are correcting a misbehavior, teaching a player how to tackle, or praising a player for good effort,

- *be positive, but honest;*
- *state it clearly and simply;*
- *say it loud enough and say it again; and*
- *be consistent.*

Be Positive, But Honest

Nothing turns people off as much as hearing someone nag all the time. Young athletes are similarly discouraged by a coach who gripes constantly. The kids on your team need encouragement because many of them doubt their ability to play football. So *look* for and *tell* your players what they did well.

On the other hand, don't cover up poor or incorrect play with false words of praise. Kids know all too well when they've fumbled or missed a tackle, and no cheerfully expressed cliché can undo their errors. What's more, if you fail to acknowledge players' mistakes, they'll think you're a phony.

State It Clearly and Simply

Positive and honest messages are good, but only if expressed directly and in words your players understand. "Beating around the bush" is ineffective and inefficient. If you ramble, your players will miss the point of

Compliment Sandwich

A good way to handle situations in which you have identified and must correct improper technique is to serve your players a "compliment sandwich."

1. Point out what the athlete did correctly.
2. Let the player know what was incorrect in the performance and instruct him how to correct it.
3. Encourage the player by reemphasizing what he did well.

your message and probably lose interest. Below are some tips for saying things clearly.

- Organize your thoughts before speaking to your athletes.
- Explain things thoroughly, but don't bore them with long-winded monologues.
- Use language that your players can understand. However, avoid trying to be "hip" by using their age group's slang words.

Say It Loud Enough and Say It Again

Trying to communicate with kids who are spread out from one end zone to the other can be difficult. So talk to your team in a voice that all members can hear and interpret.

It's okay, in fact appropriate, to soften your voice when speaking to a player individually about a personal problem. But most of the time your messages will be for all your players to hear, so make sure they can! A word of caution, however: Don't dominate the setting with a booming voice that detracts attention from players' performances.

Sometimes what you say, even if stated loud and clear, won't sink in the first time.

This may be particularly true with young athletes hearing words they don't understand.

To avoid boring repetition but still get your message across, say the same thing in a slightly different way. For instance, you might first tell your players, "Get an angle on the runner." Then, soon thereafter, remind them, "Try to meet and tackle the ball-carrier near or behind the line of scrimmage, without letting him get by you for a touchdown." The second message may get through to some players who missed it the first time around.

Send Consistent Messages

People often say things in ways that imply a different message. For example, a touch of sarcasm added to the words "way to go" sends an entirely different message than the words themselves suggest.

It is essential that you avoid sending such mixed messages. Keep the tone of your voice consistent with the words you use. And don't say something one day and contradict it the next; players will get confused.

Nonverbal Messages

Just as you should be consistent in the tone of voice and words you use, you should also keep your verbal and nonverbal messages consistent. An extreme example of failing to do this would be shaking your head, indicating disapproval, while at the same time telling a player "nice try." Which is the player to believe, your gesture or your words?

Messages can be sent nonverbally in a number of ways. Facial expressions and body language are just two of the more obvious forms of nonverbal signals that can help you when you coach.

Facial Expressions

The look on a person's face is the quickest clue to what he thinks or feels. Your players know this, so they will study your face, looking for any sign that will tell them more than the words you say. Don't try to fool them by putting on a happy or blank "mask." They'll see through it, and you'll lose credibility.

Serious, stone-faced expressions are no help to kids who need cues as to how they are performing. They will just assume you're unhappy or disinterested.

So don't be afraid to smile. A smile from a coach can boost the confidence of an unsure young athlete. Plus, a smile lets your players know that you are happy coaching them. But don't overdo it because your players won't be able to tell when you are genuinely pleased by something they've done or when you are just "putting on" a smiling face.

Body Language

How would your players think you felt if you came to practice slouched over, with head down and shoulders slumped? Tired? Bored? Unhappy? How would they think you felt if you watched them during a game with your hands on your hips, teeth clenched, and face reddened? Upset with them? Disgusted at an official? Mad at a fan?

Probably some or all of these things would enter your players' minds. That's why you should carry yourself in a pleasant, confident, and vigorous manner. Such a posture not only projects happiness with your coaching role, it also provides a good example for

your young players who may model your behavior.

Physical contact can also be a very important use of body language. A handshake, a pat on the helmet, an arm around the shoulder pads, or even a big "high five" are effective ways of showing approval, concern, affection, and joy to your players. Young, developing athletes are especially in need of this type of nonverbal message.

How Can I Improve My Receiving Skills?

Now let's examine the other half of the communication process—receiving messages. Too often people are very good senders and very poor receivers of messages; they seem to naturally enjoy hearing themselves talk more than listening to others. As a coach of young athletes it is essential that you receive their verbal and nonverbal messages effectively.

You can be a better receiver of your players' messages if you are willing to read about the keys to receiving messages and then make a strong effort to use them with your players. You'll be surprised what you've been missing.

Attention!

First you must pay attention; you must want to hear what others have to communicate to you. That's not always easy when you're busy coaching and have many things competing for your attention. But in one-to-one and team meetings with players, you must really focus on what they are telling you, both verbally and nonverbally. Not only will such focused attention help you catch every word they say, but you'll also notice their mood and physical state, and you'll get an idea of their feelings toward you and other players on the team.

Listen CARE-FULLY

How we receive messages from others, perhaps more than anything else we do, demonstrates how much we care for the sender and what that person has to tell us. If you care little for your players or have little regard for what they have to say, it will show in how you attend and listen to them.

Check yourself. Do you find your mind wandering to what you're going to do after practice while one of your players is talking to you? Do you frequently have to ask your players, "What did you say?" If so, you need to work on your receiving mechanics of attending and listening. If you find that you're missing the messages your players send, perhaps the most critical question you should ask yourself is this: Do I care?

How Do I Put It All Together?

So far we've discussed separately the sending and receiving of messages, as if a quarterback were passing a ball to a receiver. But we all know that in the game of communication, senders and receivers often switch roles several times. One person initiates the interaction by sending a message to another person, who then receives the message. The receiver then switches roles and becomes the sender by responding to the person who sent the initial message. These verbal and nonverbal responses are called *feedback*.

Your players will look to you for feedback all the time. They will want to know how you think they are performing, what you think of their ideas, and whether their efforts please you. *How* you respond will strongly affect your players. So let's take a look at a few general types of feedback and examine their possible effects.

Providing Instructions

With young players, much of your feedback will involve answering questions about how to play football. Your instructive responses to these questions should include both verbal and nonverbal feedback. The following are suggestions for giving instructional feedback:

- Keep verbal instructions simple and concise.
- Use demonstrations to provide nonverbal instructional feedback (see Unit 4).
- "Walk" players through the skill, or use a slow-motion demonstration if they are having trouble learning.

Correcting Errors

When your players perform incorrectly, you need to provide informative feedback to correct the error—and the sooner the better. And when you do correct errors, keep in mind these two principles: Use negative criticism sparingly, and keep calm.

Use Negative Criticism Sparingly

Although you may need to punish players for horseplay or dangerous activities by scolding them or temporarily removing them from activity, avoid reprimanding players for performance errors. Admonishing players for honest mistakes makes them afraid to even try. So instead, correct your players by using the positive approach. They'll enjoy playing more and you'll enjoy coaching more.

Keep Calm

Don't fly off the handle when your players make mistakes. Remember, you're coaching young and inexperienced players, not pros. You'll therefore see more incorrect than correct technique, and probably have more discipline problems than you expect. But throwing a tantrum over each error or misbehavior will only inhibit them or suggest to them the wrong kind of behavior to imitate. So let your players know that mistakes aren't the end of the world; stay cool!

Positive Feedback

Praising players when they have performed or behaved well is an effective way of getting them to repeat (or try to repeat) that behavior in the future. And positive feedback for effort is an especially effective way to motivate youngsters to work on difficult skills. So rather than shouting and providing negative feedback to a player who has made a mistake, try offering a compliment sandwich, described on page 12.

Sometimes just the way you word feedback can make it more positive than negative. For example, instead of saying, ''Don't block with your feet like that,'' you might say, ''Block with your feet shoulder-width apart.'' Then your players will be focusing on *what to do* instead of what *not* to do.

You can give positive feedback verbally and nonverbally. Telling a player, especially in front of teammates, that he has performed well is a great way to increase a kid's

Coaches, Be Positive!

Only a very small percentage of ACEP-trained coaches' behaviors are negative.

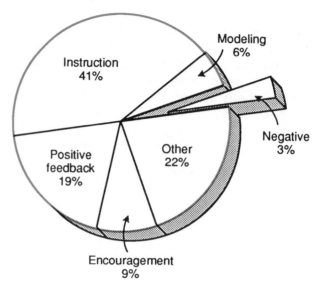

confidence. And a pat on the back or a handshake can be a very tangible way of communicating your recognition of a player's performance.

Who Else Do I Need to Communicate With?

Coaching not only involves sending and receiving messages and providing proper feedback to players, but also includes interacting with players' parents, fans, officials, and opposing coaches. Try these suggestions for communicating with each group.

Parents

A player's parents need to be assured that their child is under the direction of a coach who is both knowledgeable about football and concerned about the youngster's well-being. You can put their worries to rest by holding a preseason parent orientation meeting in which you describe your background and your approach to coaching. At this meeting you should also make it clear to parents that you are the coach, and that although you appreciate their interest, their children will be confused if you're telling the players one thing and they tell them another.

If parents contact you with a concern during the season, listen to them closely and try to offer positive responses. If you need to communicate with parents, catch them after a practice, give them a phone call, or send a note through the mail. Messages sent to parents through children are too often lost, misinterpreted, or forgotten.

Fans

The stands probably won't be overflowing at your games, but that only means that you'll more easily hear the one or two fans who criticize your coaching. When you hear something negative said about the job you're doing, don't respond. Keep calm, consider whether the message had any value, and if not, forget it. The best approach is to put away your "rabbit ears" and communicate to fans through your actions that you are a confident, competent coach.

Even if you are ready to withstand the negative comments of fans, your players may not be. Prepare them. Tell them that it is you, not the spectators, to whom they should listen. If you notice that one of your players is rattled by a fan's comment, reassure the player that your evaluation is more objective and favorable—and the one that counts.

Officials

How you communicate with officials will have a great influence on the way your players behave toward them. Therefore, you need to set an example. Greet officials with a handshake, an introduction, and perhaps some casual conversation about the upcoming contest. Indicate your respect for them before, during, and after the game.

Keep in mind that most youth football officials are volunteers or are working the games for a very nominal fee. So don't make nasty remarks, shout, or use disrespectful body gestures when an official penalizes your team. Your players will see you do it, and they'll get the idea that such behavior is appropriate. Plus, if the referee hears or sees you, the communication between the two of you will break down. In short, coach the game, don't try to call it.

Opposing Coaches

Make an effort to visit with the coach of the opposing team before the game. Perhaps the two of you can work out a special arrangement for the contest, such as matching up players of equal size and strength. During the game, don't get into a personal feud with the opposing coach. Remember, it's the kids, not the coaches, who are competing.

Summary Checklist

Now, check your coach-communication skills by answering "Yes" or "No" to the following questions.

	Yes	No
1. Are your verbal messages to your players positive and honest?	——	——
2. Do you speak loudly, clearly, and in a language your athletes understand?	——	——

(Cont.)

(continued)

		Yes	No
3.	Do you remember to repeat instructions to your players, in case they didn't hear you the first time?	____	____
4.	Are your tone of voice and your nonverbal messages consistent with the words you use?	____	____
5.	Do your facial expressions and body language express interest in and happiness with your coaching role?	____	____
6.	Are you attentive to your players and able to pick up even their small verbal and nonverbal cues?	____	____
7.	Do you really care about what your athletes say to you?	____	____
8.	Do you instruct rather than criticize when your players make errors?	____	____
9.	Are you usually positive when responding to things your athletes say and do?	____	____
10.	Do you try to communicate in a cooperative and respectful manner with players' parents, fans, officials, and opposing coaches?	____	____

If you answered "No" to any of the preceding questions, you may want to refer back to the section of the chapter where the topic was discussed. *Now* is the time to address communication problems, not when you're coaching your players.

How Do I Get My Team Ready to Play?

To coach football, you must understand the basic rules, skills, and strategies of the sport. The second part of this *Rookie Coaches Football Guide* provides the basic information you'll need to comprehend the sport.

But all the football knowledge in the world will do you little good unless you present it effectively to your players. That's why this unit is so important. In it you will learn the steps to take in teaching football skills, as well as practical guidelines for planning your season and individual practices.

How Do I Teach Football Skills?

Many people believe that the only qualification needed to coach is to have played the sport. It's helpful to have played, but there is much more to coaching successfully. And even if you haven't played football, you can still teach the skills of the sport effectively using this IDEA:

I—Introduce the skill.

D—Demonstrate the skill.

E—Explain the skill.

A—Attend to players practicing the skill.

Introduce the Skill

Players, especially if they're young and inexperienced, need to know what skill they are learning and why they are learning it. You should, therefore, take these three steps every time you introduce a skill to your players:

1. Get your players' attention.
2. Name the skill.
3. Explain the importance of the skill.

Get Your Players' Attention

Because youngsters are easily distracted, use some method to get their attention. Some coaches use interesting news items or stories. Others use jokes. And others simply project an enthusiasm that gets their players to listen. Whatever method you use, speak slightly above the normal volume and look your players in the eye when you speak. Also arrange the players in two or three evenly spaced rows and facing you, not some source of distraction. Ask the players to get on one knee. Then check that all can see and hear you before you begin.

Name the Skill

Although you might mention other common names for the skill, decide which one you'll use, and stick with it. This will help avoid confusion and enhance communication among your players. For example, choose either "swing pass" or "flare" as the term for the short quick pass to a back, and use it consistently.

Explain the Importance of the Skill

Although the importance of a skill may be apparent to you, your players may be less able to see how the skill will help them become better football players. Offer them a reason for learning the skill, and describe

how the skill relates to more advanced skills. For instance, explain that the swing pass is an effective tool against a hard-rushing defense. Mention also that, because it is a relatively short throw, it is easier to complete than a throw downfield. Then explain that the swing pass can also be used as a secondary option when the primary receiver is covered.

The most difficult aspect of coaching is this: Coaches must learn to let athletes learn. Sport skills should be taught so they have meaning to the child, not just meaning to the coach.

Rainer Martens, ACEP Founder

Demonstrate the Skill

The demonstration step is the most important part of teaching a football skill to young players who may have never done anything that closely resembles it. They need a picture, not just words. They need to *see* how the skill is performed.

If you are unable to perform the skill correctly, it may be too advanced for your players. If the skill is appropriate, and you still need someone else to demonstrate, have an assistant coach or someone skilled in football perform the demonstration. A high school varsity player would be an excellent choice, because the young players will identify with him. These tips will help make your demonstrations more effective:

- Use correct form.
- Demonstrate the skill several times.
- Slow the skill down, if possible, during one or two performances so players can see every movement involved in the skill.
- Perform the skill at different angles so your players can get a full perspective of it.
- Demonstrate the skill to both the right and left sides.

Explain the Skill

Players learn more effectively if they're given a brief explanation of the skill along with the demonstration. Use simple terms

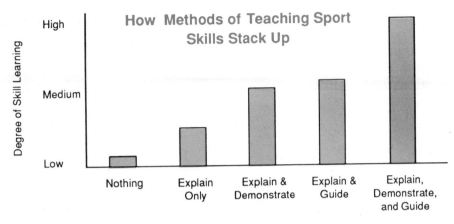

to describe the skill and, if possible, relate the skill to previously learned skills. Ask your players if they understand your description. If one of them looks confused, have him explain the skill back to you.

Complex skills often are better understood if they are explained in more manageable parts. For instance, if you want to teach your players how to tackle a ballcarrier when a blocker is coming at them, you might take the following steps:

1. Show them a correct performance of the entire skill and explain its function in football.
2. Break down the skill and point out its component parts to your players.
3. Have players perform each of the component skills you have already taught them, such as getting in their stance, firing off the ball, identifying where the play is going and who has the ball, fending off the blocker, pursuing the ballcarrier, and making the tackle.
4. After players have demonstrated their ability to perform the separate parts of the skill in sequence, reexplain the entire skill.
5. Have them practice the skill.

Attend to Players Practicing the Skill

If the skill you selected was within your players' abilities and you have done an effective job of introducing, demonstrating, and explaining it, your players should be ready to attempt the skill. Some players may need to be physically guided through the

movements during their first few attempts at the skill.

For example, some players may need your hands-on help to get their feet in the correct position for their three-point stance. "Walking" unsure athletes through the skill in this way will help them gain confidence to perform the skill on their own.

Your teaching duties don't end when all your athletes have demonstrated that they understand how to perform the skill. In fact, a significant part of your teaching will involve observing closely the hit-and-miss, trial performances of your players.

As you observe players' efforts in drills and activities, offer positive, corrective feedback in the form of the "compliment sandwich" described in Unit 3. If a player performs the skill properly, acknowledge it and offer praise. Keep in mind that your feedback will have a great influence on your players' motivation to practice and improve their performance.

Remember, too, that young players need individual instruction. So set aside a time before, during, or after practice to give them individual help.

What Planning Do I Need to Do?

Beginning coaches often make the mistake of showing up for the first practice with no particular plan in mind. These coaches find that their practices are unorganized, their players are frustrated and inattentive, and the amount and quality of their instruction is limited. Planning is essential to successful teaching *and* coaching. And it doesn't begin on the way to practice!

Preseason Planning

Effective coaches begin planning well before the start of the season. Among the preseason measures that will make the season more enjoyable, successful, and safe for you and your players are the following:

- Familiarize yourself with the sport organization you are involved in, especial-

ly its philosophy and goals regarding youth sport.

- Examine the availability of facilities, equipment, instructional aids, and other materials needed for practices and games.
- Check to see if you have liability insurance to cover you when one of your players is hurt (see Unit 5). If you don't, get some.
- Establish your coaching priorities regarding having fun, developing players' skills, and winning.
- Select and meet with your assistant coaches to discuss the philosophy, goals, team rules, and plans for the season.
- Register players for the team. Have them complete a player information form and obtain medical clearance forms, if required.
- Institute an injury-prevention program for your players.
- Hold a parent-athlete-coach meeting to inform parents of your background, philosophy, goals, and instructional approach. Also, give a brief overview of the league's rules and football rules, terms, and strategies to familiarize parents with the sport.

You may be surprised at the number of things you should do even before the first practice. But if you address them during the preseason, the season will be much more enjoyable and productive for you and your players.

In-Season Planning

Your choice of activities during the season should be based on players' maturity and whether the activities will help your players develop physical and mental skills, knowledge of rules and game tactics, sportsmanship, and love for the sport. All of these goals are important, but we'll focus on the skills and tactics of football to give you an idea of how to itemize your objectives.

Goal Setting

What you plan to do during the season must be reasonable for the maturity and skill level of your players. In terms of football skills and tactics, you should teach young players the basics and move on to more complex activities only after they have mastered these easier techniques and strategies.

To begin the season, your instructional goals might include the following:

- Players will be able to get into a correct stance for any position they might play.
- Players will be able to use proper footwork for the positions they play.
- Players will be able to demonstrate correct positioning for effective blocking.
- Players will be able to demonstrate proper and safe tackling techniques.
- Players will be able to demonstrate knowledge of the rules of football.
- Players will be able to line up in the correct position on offense and defense.
- Players will be able to demonstrate teamwork throughout the season.
- Players will be able to demonstrate their preparation for practices and games during those events.
- Players will be able to demonstrate a basic understanding of offensive and defensive strategies.
- Players will be able to demonstrate good sportsmanship at all times.
- Players will increase their enjoyment of football and develop an interest in learning more about the game.

Organizing

After you've defined the skills and tactics you want your players to learn during the season, you can plan how to teach them to your players in practices. But be flexible! If your players are having difficulty learning a skill or tactic, take some extra time until they get the hang of it—even if that means moving back your schedule. After all, if your players are unable to perform the fundamental skills, they'll never execute the more complex skills you have scheduled for them.

Still, it helps to have a plan for progressing players through skills during the season. The sample plan in Appendix B shows how you might schedule your instruction in an organized and progressive manner. If this is your first coaching experience, you may wish to follow the plan as it stands. If you have some previous experience, you may want to modify the schedule to better fit the needs of your team.

What Makes Up a Good Practice?

A good instructional plan makes practice preparation much easier. Have players work on more important and less difficult goals in early-season practice sessions. And make sure that players master basic skills before moving on to more advanced ones.

It is helpful to establish *one objective* for each practice, but try to include a *variety of activities* related to that objective. This can make an otherwise boring football practice fun.

For example, although your primary objective might be to improve players' tackling ability, you can do several drills that simultaneously develop the opposing players' offensive skills.

By using several different drills designed to enhance tackling skills, you can keep players' interest high. And, to inject further variety into your practices, vary the order of the activities you schedule for players to perform.

In general, we recommend that each of your practices include the following:

- *Warm up*
- *Teach and practice new skills*
- *Practice previously taught skills*
- *Practice under gamelike conditions*
- *Cool down*
- *Evaluate*

Warm Up

As you're checking the roster and announcing the performance objectives for the practice, your players should be preparing their bodies for vigorous activity. A 5- to 10-minute period of easy-paced activities (e.g., three-quarter-speed running around the field, stretching, and calisthenics) should be sufficient for youngsters to limber their muscles and reduce the risk of injury.

Practice Previously Taught Skills

Devote part of each practice to having players work on the fundamental skills they already know. But remember, kids like variety. So organize and modify drills to keep everyone involved and interested. Praise and encourage players when you notice improvement, and offer individual assistance to those who need help.

Teach and Practice New Skills

Gradually build on your players' existing skills by giving them something new to practice each session. The proper method for teaching sport skills is described on pages 19 to 22. Refer to those pages if you have any questions about teaching new skills, or if you want to evaluate your teaching approach periodically during the season.

Practice Under Gamelike Conditions

Competition among teammates during practices prepares players for actual games and informs young athletes about their abilities relative to those of their peers. Youngsters also seem to have more fun in competitive activities.

You can create contestlike conditions by using competitive drills, modified games, and scrimmages (see Units 7 and 8). However, consider the following guidelines before introducing competition into your practices.

- All players should have an equal opportunity to participate.
- Match players by ability and physical maturity.
- Make certain players can execute fundamental skills before they compete in groups.
- Emphasize improving performance, not winning, in every game.
- Give players room to make mistakes by avoiding constant evaluation of their performances.

Cool Down

Each practice should wind down with a 5- to 10-minute period of light exercise, including jogging, performance of simple skills, and some stretching. The cool-down allows athletes' bodies to return to the resting state and avoid stiffness, and affords you an opportunity to review the practice.

Evaluate

At the end of practice spend a few minutes with your players reviewing how well the session accomplished the objective you had set. Even if your evaluation is negative, show optimism for future practices and send players off on an upbeat note.

How Do I Put a Practice Together?

Simply knowing the six practice components is not enough. You must also be able to arrange those components into a logical progression and fit them into a time schedule. Now, using your instructional goals as a guide for selecting what skills to have your players work on, try to plan several football practices you might conduct. The following example should help you get started.

Sample Practice Plan

Performance Objective. Players will be able to use proper tackling techniques.

Component	Time	Activity or drill
Warm up	10 min	Easy running Stretching Calisthenics
Teach	15 min	Straight-on tackling Angle tackling Open-field tackling
Practice previously taught skills	25 min	Defensive positioning Blocking Fending off blockers
Practice under gamelike conditions	20 min	Form Tackling drill Sideline Tackling drill Small-sided scrimmage
Cool down and evaluate	10 min	3/4-speed offensive plays Stretching Coach's comments

Summary Checklist

During your football season, check your teaching and planning skills periodically. As you gain more coaching experience, you should be able to answer "Yes" to each of the following.

When you teach football skills to your players, do you

____ arrange the players so all can see and hear?

____ introduce the skill clearly and explain its importance?

____ demonstrate the skill properly several times?

____ explain the skill simply and accurately?

____ attend closely to players practicing the skill?

____ offer corrective, positive feedback or praise after observing players' attempts at the skill?

When you plan, do you remember to plan for

____ preseason events like player registration, liability protection, use of facilities, and parent orientation?

____ season goals such as the development of players' physical skills, mental skills, sportsmanship, and enjoyment?

____ practice components such as warming up, practicing previously taught skills, teaching and practicing new skills, practicing under gamelike conditions, cooling down, and evaluating?

UNIT 5

What About Safety?

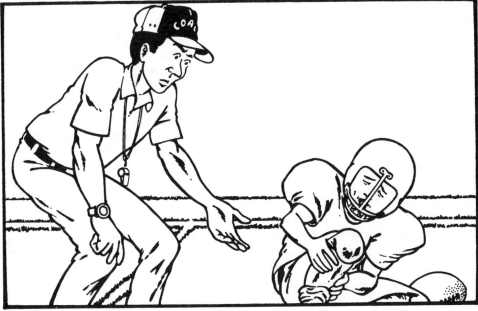

Your fullback breaks free through a huge hole in the line, and it appears that he has daylight all the way to the end zone. Suddenly, a linebacker comes from nowhere and makes a crushing tackle on the runner. Although momentarily pleased with the yardage gained on the play, you quickly become concerned when you see that the ballcarrier is not able to get back on his feet. He seems to be in pain. What do you do?

One of the least pleasant aspects of coaching is observing players get hurt. Fortunately, coaches can institute many preventive measures to reduce the risk. But in spite of such efforts, injury remains a reality of sport participation. And consequently, you must be prepared to pro-vide first aid when injuries occur. This unit will describe how you can

- create the safest possible environment for your players,
- provide emergency first aid to players when they get hurt, and
- protect yourself from injury liability.

How Do I Keep My Players From Getting Hurt?

Injuries can occur because of poor preventive measures. So, as part of your planning (described in Unit 4), include these important steps to give your players the best possible chance to participate injury-free:

- *Preseason physical examination*
- *Physical conditioning*
- *Equipment and facilities inspection*
- *Matching players by physical maturity and warning of inherent risks*
- *Proper supervision and record keeping*
- *Sufficient hydration*
- *Warming up and cooling down*

Preseason Physical Examination

In the absence of severe injury or ongoing illness, your players should have a physical examination every 2 years. If a player has a known complication, a physician's consent should be obtained before participation is allowed. You should also have players' parents or guardians sign a participation agreement form and a release form to allow their child to be treated in the case of an emergency.

Physical Conditioning

Muscles, tendons, and ligaments unaccustomed to vigorous physical activity are prone to injury. Add to this the physical contact between players pushing and pulling in different directions, and it's apparent why you must prepare your athletes' bodies to withstand the physical demands of playing football. An effective conditioning program for football would include running sprints and strength training. Stretching and agility drills should be used to complement these activities.

Make conditioning drills and activities fun. Include a skill component, such as firing out of a stance, running pass patterns, or returning kickoffs, to prevent players from becoming bored or looking upon the conditioning process as "work."

Equipment and Facilities Inspection

Another means to prevent injuries is to check the quality and fit of the equipment and uniforms worn by your players. Slick-soled, poor-fitting, or unlaced football shoes

---

INFORMED CONSENT FORM

I hereby give my permission for _____ to participate in

_____ during the athletic season beginning in 199___. Further, I authorize the school to provide emergency treatment of an injury to or illness of my child if qualified medical personnel consider treatment necessary *and* perform the treatment. This authorization is granted only if I cannot be reached and a reasonable effort has been made to do so.

Date _____   Parent or guardian _____

Address _____   Phone ( )_____

Family physician _____   Phone ( )_____

Pre-existing medical conditions (e.g., allergies or chronic illnesses) _____

_____

Other(s) to also contact in case of emergency _____

Relationship to child _____   Phone ( )_____

My child and I are aware that participating in _____ is a potentially hazardous activity. I assume all risks associated with participation in this sport, including but not limited to falls, contact with other participants, the effects of the weather, traffic, and other reasonable risk conditions associated with the sport. All such risks to my child are known and understood by me.

I understand this informed consent form and agree to its conditions on behalf of my child.

Child's signature _____   Date _____

Parent's signature _____   Date _____

are a knee or ankle injury waiting to happen. Make sure your players' shoes have the appropriate-sized studs, are the proper size for their feet, and are double-tied to prevent self-inflicted "shoestring tackles." Two pairs of socks are better than one for preventing blisters.

The pants, pads, jerseys, and helmets your players wear will probably be supplied by your local youth sport program. Check the quality of all equipment and uniforms before fitting them to the kids on your team. After distributing good, proper-fitting equipment, show players how to put on every part of their uniforms. Advise them to wear an undershirt beneath their shoulder pads to reduce the chance of skin irritations.

Make certain that each player on the field has a mouthpiece in place at all times. And tell your athletes that the only time their chin straps should ever be unsnapped is when they are on the sidelines.

Remember to examine regularly the field on which your players practice and play. Remove hazards, report conditions you cannot remedy, and request maintenance as necessary.

Matching Athletes by Maturity and Warning of Inherent Risks

Children of the same age may differ in height and weight by up to 6 inches and 50 pounds. In football, the advantage of size and maturity is critical. It is not fair or safe to pit an underdeveloped young athlete against a player whose physique belongs in the NFL.

Try to give smaller, less mature children a better chance to succeed and avoid injury, and larger children more of a challenge. Playing experience, ability, and emotional maturity are also important factors to keep in mind when matching players on the football field.

Matching helps protect you from certain liability concerns. But you also must warn players of the inherent risks involved in playing football, because "failure to warn" is one of the most successful arguments in lawsuits against coaches. So, thoroughly explain the inherent risks of football, and make sure each player knows, understands, and appreciates those risks.

The preseason parent-athlete-coach meeting is a good opportunity to explain the risks of the sport to parents and players. It is also a good occasion to have both the players and their parents sign waivers releasing you from liability in the event of an injury. Such waivers do not discharge you of responsibility for your players' well-being, but they are recommended by lawyers.

Proper Supervision and Record Keeping

With youngsters, your mere presence in the area of play is not enough; you must actively plan and direct team activities and closely observe and evaluate players' participation. You're the watchdog responsible for their welfare. So if you notice a player limping or grimacing, give him a rest and examine the extent of the injury.

As a coach, you're also required to enforce the rules of the sport, prohibit dangerous horseplay, and hold practices only under safe weather conditions. These specific supervisory activities will make the play environment safer for your players and help protect you from liability should an injury occur.

For further protection, keep records of your season plans, practice plans, and players' injuries. Season and practice plans come in handy when you need evidence that players have been taught certain skills, and accurate, detailed accident report forms offer protection against unfounded lawsuits. Ask

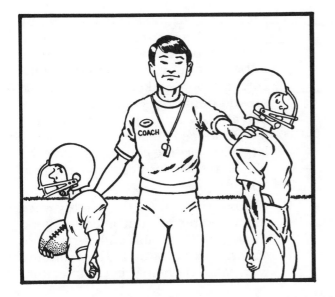

for these forms from the organization to which you belong. And hold onto these records for several years so an "old football injury" of a former player doesn't come back to haunt you.

Sufficient Hydration

You know how hot and sticky it can get out on a football field when you're wearing a helmet and all that padding. Add a lot of activity and competition, and body temperature can really rise.

So football players need a ready supply of cool water to keep from dehydrating. And they may need reminders from you to take a break and wet their whistles, because the signal in the brain that tells us we need fluids lags far behind our actual requirement.

Warming Up and Cooling Down

Although young bodies are generally very limber, they can get tight from inactivity. Therefore, a warm-up period of approximately 10 minutes before each practice is strongly recommended. Warm-up should address each muscle group and get the heart rate elevated in preparation for strenuous activity. Easy running and stretching, followed by more vigorous calisthenics like jumping jacks, sit-ups, and push-ups, is a common sequence.

As practice is winding down, slow players' heart rate with some moderate then easy-paced activities. Continuous, half-speed execution of all your running plays can be a good way to cool down and review simultaneously. Before you call it a day, arrange for a 5- or 10-minute period of easy stretching to help players avoid stiff muscles and make them less tight before the next practice.

What If One of My Players Gets Hurt?

No matter how good and thorough your prevention program, injuries will occur. And, when injury does strike, chances are you will be the one in charge. The severity and nature of the injury will determine how actively involved you'll be in treating the injury. But regardless of how seriously a player is hurt, it is your responsibility to know what steps to take. So let's look at how you can provide *basic* emergency care to your injured athletes.

ACEP Fact

The injury rate in youth football is approximately 15%.

Minor Injuries

Although no injury seems minor to the person experiencing it, most injuries are neither life-threatening nor severe enough to restrict participation. When such injuries occur, you can take an active role in their initial treatment.

Scrapes and Cuts

When a player has an open wound, first put on a pair of disposable surgical gloves or some other effective blood barrier. Then follow these three steps:

1. Stop, slow, or moderate bleeding by applying direct pressure with a clean dressing to the wound and elevating it. *Do not* remove the dressing if it becomes blood-soaked. Instead, place an additional dressing on top of the one already in place. If a foreign object is lodged inside, the wound is large, or bleeding continues, have the player receive professional medical attention.

2. Cleanse the wound thoroughly once the bleeding is controlled. A good rinsing with a forceful stream of water, and perhaps light scrubbing with soap will help prevent infection.

3. Protect the wound with sterile gauze or a bandage. If the player can participate without risk of further damage to the wound, also apply protective padding over the injured area.

For bloody noses not associated with serious facial injury, have the athlete sit and lean slightly forward. Then pinch the player's nostrils shut. If the bleeding continues after several minutes or if the athlete has a history of nosebleeds, seek medical assistance.

ACEP Fact

The area most frequently injured by children participating in youth football is the upper body. Fractures, sprains, bruises, and strains are the most common problems.

Sprains and Strains

The physical demands of football practices and games often result in injury to the ligaments (sprains), and sometimes to the muscles or tendons (strains). When your players suffer minor sprains or strains, immediately apply the RICE method of injury care.

Bumps and Bruises

Inevitably, football players make contact with each other and with the playing field. And if the force of a body part at impact is great enough, a bump or bruise will result. Many players will continue playing with such sore spots. But if the bump or bruise is large and painful, you should act appropriately. Enact the RICE formula for injury care and monitor the injury. If swelling, discoloration, and pain have lessened, the player may resume participation with protective padding; if not, the player should be examined by a physician.

Serious Injuries

Head and spine injuries, fractures, and injuries that cause a player to lose consciousness are among a class of injuries that you cannot and *should not try to treat* yourself. But you *should plan* what you'll do if such an injury occurs. And your plan should include the following guidelines for action:

- Obtain the phone number and ensure the availability of nearby emergency care units.
- Assign an assistant coach or another *adult* the responsibility of contacting

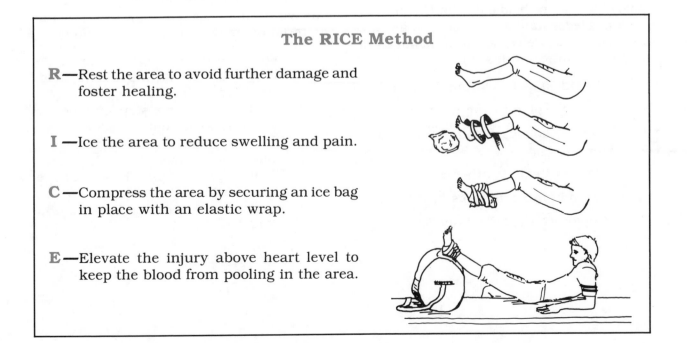

The RICE Method

R—Rest the area to avoid further damage and foster healing.

I—Ice the area to reduce swelling and pain.

C—Compress the area by securing an ice bag in place with an elastic wrap.

E—Elevate the injury above heart level to keep the blood from pooling in the area.

emergency medical help upon your request.

- *Do not move* the injured athlete.
- Calm the injured athlete and keep others away from him as much as possible.
- Evaluate whether the athlete's breathing is stopped or irregular, and, if necessary, clear the airway with your fingers.
- Administer artificial respiration if breathing has stopped.
- Administer cardiopulmonary resuscitation (CPR), or have a trained individual administer it, if the athlete's circulation has stopped.
- Remain with the athlete until medical personnel arrive.

ACEP Fact

About 5% of all youth football injuries are serious, requiring restriction from activity for at least 7 days.

How Do I Protect Myself?

When one of your players is injured, naturally your first concern is his well-being. Your feelings for children, after all, are what made you decide to coach. Unfortunately, there is something else that you must consider: Can you be held liable for the injury?

From a legal standpoint, a coach has nine duties to fulfill. We've discussed all but planning (see Unit 4) in this unit.

1. Provide a safe environment.
2. Properly plan the activity.
3. Provide adequate and proper equipment.
4. Match or equate athletes.
5. Warn of inherent risks in the sport.
6. Supervise the activity closely.

7. Evaluate athletes for injury or incapacity.
8. Know emergency care and basic first aid procedures.
9. Keep adequate records.

In addition to fulfilling these nine legal duties, you should check your insurance coverage to make sure your present policy will protect you from liability.

Summary Self-Test

Now that you've read how to make your coaching experience safe for your players and yourself, test your knowledge of the material by answering these questions:

1. What are six injury-prevention measures you can institute to try to keep your players from getting hurt?
2. What is the three-step emergency care process for cuts?
3. What method of treatment is best for minor sprains and strains?
4. What steps can you take to manage serious injuries?
5. What are the nine legal duties of a coach?

UNIT 6

What Do I Need to Know About Football?

Football is perhaps the most popular sport in the United States. Television ratings for National Football League games are higher than for any other sporting event. At the college level, many football teams draw more than 50,000 fans to each game. And hundreds of thousands of high school athletes practice and work out year-round, making interscholastic football more competitive, specialized, and sophisticated than ever before.

The scene is somewhat different in organized youth football, though the sport means just as much to the participants. Youth football gives many kids their first experience with uniforms, rules and officials to enforce them, striped and marked fields of play, and spectators. An even bigger change from their neighborhood pickup games is that they now have someone coaching them—you!

Coaching Youth Football

Because of football's popularity in this country, you probably watched or played the sport for several years before you became a coach. What you learned in any previous spectating, playing, and coaching experiences will help. But it does not ensure that you will be an effective youth football coach.

In many ways, coaching a youth football team is more difficult than coaching in the NFL. Among your biggest challenges are helping your players

- learn the game,
- participate as safely as possible, and
- have as much fun as they would have if you weren't around.

This unit as well as Units 7 and 8 of *Rookie Coaches Football Guide* will help you face these challenges. Read, learn, and use the information so you can be the kind of coach your players want and deserve.

Field of Play

You probably won't have a lot to say about the facility where your team practices and plays. However, it is your duty to inspect the facility before each practice session and game. If you spot any problems, correct those you can, and ask league administrators to correct those you cannot remedy.

Your field won't look much like the manicured, professionally chalked and painted carpets you see on televised games. And don't be surprised if it also looks a little smaller than usual. Most youth programs follow Pop Warner Football's guidelines for fields, with 80 yards between goal lines and 40 yards between sidelines (see Figure 6.1). Some programs start players on even smaller, 60-yard × 30-yard fields.

Ball

Just as the field is reduced to match players' development, so too is the size of the ball (see

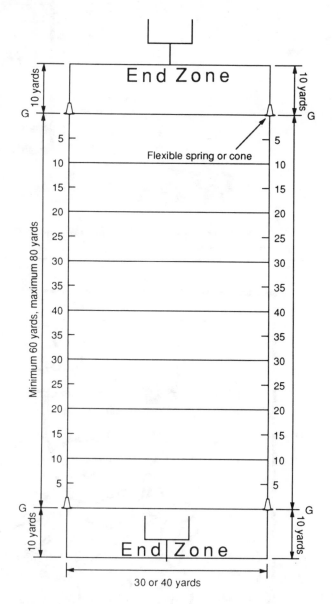

Figure 6.1   Regulation football field.

Table 6.1). Your league will probably distribute to all teams a certain size and brand of ball to use throughout the season. The ball will have a set of laces and a leather, rubber, or plastic surface. Check the air pressure of the inflated rubber bladder inside to make sure it agrees with the pressure amount designated on the ball's exterior.

Protective Equipment and Uniform

The physical nature of football requires that players wear protective gear. These items include the helmet, the mouth guard, shoul-

Table 6.1 Pop Warner Football Designated Age-Group Divisions and Ball Dimensions

Age group	Divisions	Football dimensions (inches)
7-9	Mighty Mites	10 1/4–10 1/2
8-10	Junior Pee Wees	
9-11	Pee Wees	
10-12	Junior Midgets	10 5/8–10 3/4
11-13	Midgets	
12-14	Junior Bantams	
14	Bantams	11–11 1/2 (regulation)

Figure 6.2 It is important that each player wears proper-fitting equipment:

1. *Shoulder pads.* Body padding should not extend beyond tip of shoulder—neck area should fit snugly when arms are extended over head.

2. *Helmet.* Must fit snugly around head and in jaw section—head should be in contact with crown suspension when front edge is approximately one inch above the eyebrow.

3. *Clothing.* Jersey should fit close to body and always be tucked in pants to hold shoulder pad in place—pants should hug body to keep thigh and knee guards in place.

4. *Girdle pads.* Hip pads must cover point of hip and give proper lower spine protection.

5. *Thigh and knee pads.* Must be the proper size and inserted properly into the lining of player's pants.

6. *Shoes.* Cleats should be inspected regularly to insure "even wear" and assure stability; proper width very important; upper should never "overrun" outsole.

der pads, girdle pads, thigh pads, knee pads, and shoes.

Examine the condition of each item you distribute to players. Also check that the pieces of equipment they furnish for themselves meet acceptable standards.

In addition, it is important that each piece of equipment is fit to the player. Check that each athlete on your team is outfitted properly. That means following the guidelines in Figure 6.2 for fitting a football uniform to a player.

You may have to demonstrate to players how to put on each piece of equipment. Otherwise, expect some of them to show up for the first practice with their shoulder pads on backward and their thigh pads upside down.

Shaping a mouth guard is also a mystery to most youngsters. Although these plastic mouthpieces come with easy-to-follow directions, your players may need further guidance. Take some time to explain the heating and shaping process. Just being on a real football field will give some young players lumps in their throats; they don't need to be choking on a cumbersome mouth guard at the same time.

The helmet is the most commonly misused piece of football equipment. So before distributing helmets to your players, explain very clearly that a helmet is a protective covering, *not* a weapon. If you spot a player using the helmet as a battering device, take him aside and demonstrate the correct, heads-up technique.

How the Game Is Played

When the game begins, the ball is put in play by a kickoff. A player on one team kicks the ball from a designated yard line off a tee toward the opponent's goal line. A player on either team can field the ball after it travels

10 yards downfield. If, as usually happens, a player on the receiving team gains possession, that player tries to advance the ball as far as possible toward the kicking team's goal line. The kicking team tries to *tackle* the ballcarrier as close to the receiving team's goal as possible. When the tackle is made or the ballcarrier runs out of bounds, the ball is whistled dead and play is momentarily stopped.

The point at which play resumes is called the *line of scrimmage*. The line of scrimmage stretches from one sideline to the other, passing through the point of the ball nearest the defense. The team with the ball is called the offense; the opposing team is the defense. In 11-man football, the offensive team must begin each play with at least seven players lined up on the line of scrimmage, facing the defense. Each play starts when one of these linemen, the center, snaps the ball to a teammate, typically the quarterback.

The offense is allowed four plays, or *downs*, to advance the football 10 yards toward the opponent's goal line. If successful, the offense is given a new set of downs and can maintain possession until it

- is stopped by the defense and has to *punt*, typically on fourth down;
- turns the ball over to the defense via a *fumble*, *interception*, or a failure to gain 10 yards in four attempts;
- attempts a *field goal*; or
- scores a *touchdown*.

Team Objectives

The primary objective of the offensive team is to score, although many coaches also want their offenses to maintain possession of the ball for as long as possible. By doing so, they reduce the number of chances that the opposing team's offense has to score (see What's the Score?).

The defensive team's main objective is to prevent the offense from scoring. In addition, the defense tries to make the offensive team give up possession of the ball as far away as possible from the goal line it is defending.

Offenses and defenses have many strategic options available to accomplish these objec-

What's the Score?

Here's the number of points awarded to teams that successfully execute these plays.

Play	Points	Description
Touchdown	6	Player in control of ball touches vertical plane of opponent's goal line
Field Goal	3	Placekick or dropkick from scrimmage that, without touching the ground, goes through uprights of goal
Point After Touchdown*	2	One placekick, run, or pass play from scrimmage beginning at opponent's 3-yard line. Points are awarded when kick goes through uprights of goal or team breaks vertical plane of goal line with the ball
Safety	2	Offensive player is tackled or loses ball out of bounds in his own end zone

*In Pop Warner Football, 2 points (instead of 1) are awarded for successfully kicked PATs to encourage the development of kicking skills in young players.

tives. Read Unit 8 for information on how to teach your team basic offensive and defensive tactics.

What Football Rules Should I Know?

Football rules are designed to make the game run smoothly and safely and to prevent either team from gaining an unfair advantage. Throw out the rules, and a football game quickly turns into a chaotic and dangerous competition where size, brute strength, and speed dominate.

Your league should already have rules concerning acceptable height and weight maximums and minimums for players. Even so, make sure your kids are matched up against opponents with similar physiques and skills. Discourage players from cutting weight to be eligible for your team. And, if you spot a mismatch during a game, talk with the opposing coach to see if you can cooperate and correct the problem.

Your league will also specify the length of your games. Typically, youth football games consist of four 8- or 10-minute quarters. The clock is stopped when

- there is a change of possession,
- the ball goes out of bounds,
- an incomplete pass is thrown,
- the yard markers need to be advanced after a team gains 10 yards for a first down,
- a player is injured and officials call a time-out,
- a team scores, and
- a team calls a time-out.

You will be given two or three time-outs in each half. Use them wisely, and not just for talking strategy. Remember, although the games may seem short to you, young players can get fatigued easily. So in addition to substituting regularly, call a time-out when you see that your team is tired.

Playing by the Rules

You are in a position to teach your players more than simply to obey the rules of the game. As a coach, you have a responsibility to teach them only those techniques that are safe.

For example, it's one thing to discourage spearing on defense; that's against the rules. But it's also essential to teach young players *never* to lead with their heads when blocking or running. Kicking or striking an opponent or jumping on the pile at the conclusion of a play is not acceptable. Also, teach your players not to grasp an opponent's face mask because doing so can cause serious neck injuries. If you fail to do so, you are directly contributing not only to the next penalty one of your players commits, but also to the next injury one of your players suffers.

Football is a contact, perhaps collision, sport. If the game is played according to the letter *and* spirit of the rules, youngsters can participate safely. Make certain that your players do. The proper football techniques to teach young football players are described in Unit 7. Techniques that you should not tolerate are listed under Football No Nos.

Football No Nos

It's inevitable that your players will violate minor rules during practices and games; even pros go offsides now and then. But make clear to your players that some actions are *unacceptable* on the football field. These are typically called unsportsmanlike conduct penalties or personal fouls.

- Tripping
- Face masking (pulling on an opponent's face mask)
- Blocking or tackling with a closed fist
- Spearing (tackling with top of helmet)
- Swearing
- Taunting
- Fighting
- Clipping (blocking a player in the back)
- Clotheslining (knocking a player down with a blow to the head or/neck)

Promote good sportsmanship along with the use of proper fundamentals. Encourage defenders to help opponents up after a tackle. And ask ballcarriers to hand the ball to the referee or leave it on the ground where they are tackled. The official will appreciate such behavior, and so will the players' parents, league administrators, and players' future coaches.

Common Rule Infractions

Pop Warner Football and your local youth football program have rule books available for your use. Take the time to study and learn the ins and outs, then teach the rules to your football team.

Although no youth football team will perform penalty-free, teach your players to avoid recurring penalties. By instilling this discipline, you'll help them enjoy more success, both as individuals and as a team.

Here is a brief list of common infractions football players commit.

Offsides: Defensive player in or beyond the neutral zone when the ball is snapped

Encroachment: Offensive player in or beyond the neutral zone before the ball is snapped

Illegal procedure: Failure of the offensive team to have seven players on the line of scrimmage (in 11-man football); the offensive team having more than one player in motion or a player moving toward the line of scrimmage before the snap

Delay of game: Offensive team taking more than 25 seconds to snap the ball after the referee has marked it ready for play

Holding: Any player using the arms to hook or lock up an opponent to impede his movement; an offensive player extending the arms outside his body frame to grab an opponent

Pass interference (defensive):   Defensive player making contact with an eligible receiver who is beyond the neutral zone, with the intent of impeding the offensive player trying to catch a catchable forward pass

As you teach your athletes to play with discipline and to avoid such rule violations, remember that you are their model. Players will reflect the discipline that you display in teaching them in practices and coaching them from the sidelines during games. So show respect for the rules, and don't shrug off game infractions or personal misconduct. And provide a great example by communicating respectfully with the individuals who officiate your games.

Officiating

Football rules are enforced by a crew of officials on the field. From the opening coin toss to the final horn, officials see to it that the game is conducted fairly.

In youth football, as many as seven or as few as two officials may work the games. The referee is the official who controls the game, marking the ball ready for play; signaling penalties, time-outs, and first downs; and communicating with team captains and coaches. Appendix A shows the referees' signals for most common rule infractions.

If you have a concern about how a game is being officiated, address the referee respectfully. Do so immediately if at any time you feel that the officiating jeopardizes the safety of your players.

Player Positions

Give your young athletes a chance to play a variety of positions, on both offense and defense. If they're exposed to different positions, they'll become better all-around players and will probably stay a lot more interested in the sport. Plus, they'll have a better understanding of the many skills and tactics used in the game. They will also better appreciate the efforts of their teammates who play positions they find difficult.

Offensive Positions

Figure 6.3 illustrates a basic 11-player offensive alignment. Here's a brief outline of the

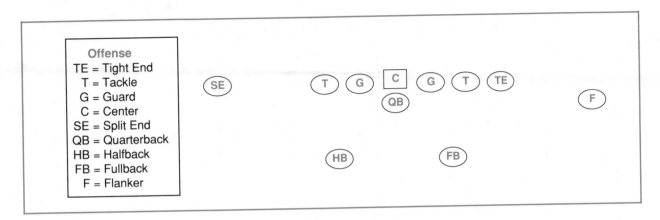

Figure 6.3 Offensive team alignment.

desired attributes and responsibilities of players at each position.

Offensive Linemen

Ideally, you'll be able to put big, strong, and quick athletes into the center, guard, and tackle positions. These players must block and open up holes for ballcarriers to run through. And, when a pass play is called, they must protect the quarterback from opposing linemen.

Receivers

Another player who has important blocking duties is the tight end, positioned on the line of scrimmage, next to (within 3 yards of) either tackle. The tight end must be strong enough to block a defensive end, yet speedy enough to get open on pass routes.

The two other receiver positions are the flanker and the split end, or wide receiver. Speed and agility, along with a great catching ability, are the qualities to look for in filling these spots. The flanker can be positioned on either side, off the line of scrimmage, whereas the split end is 8 to 10 yards outside the opposite tackle and up on the line. When the flanker is on the split end side, he is referred to as the slot. When a team positions a split end and flanker on each side of the line, it's called a double slot.

Quarterback

Lined up directly behind the center to receive the snap, the quarterback is the "field general" of the offense. The quarterback calls the plays in the huddle, barks out the snap count at the line of scrimmage, and then, after taking the snap, hands the ball off, runs with it, or passes it.

At this position you'll want to put a good communicator and good athlete who can handle many responsibilities. And, to complete your wish list, the quarterback will have an excellent throwing arm.

Running Backs

Most teams use a two-back set, either a deuce formation like the one shown in Figure 6.3 or an I formation where the backs line up in a straight line behind the quarterback.

Often, one running back is called a fullback and the other a halfback. The fullback has more blocking responsibilities and is expected to pick up short yardage when needed. Therefore, you'll want a strong, fairly fast, and dependable player at this position. The halfback (called the tailback in the I formation) is the primary ballcarrier. Speed and agility to outrun and outmaneuver would-be tacklers are very desirable attributes for a halfback.

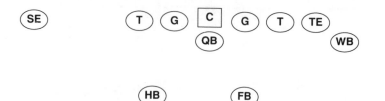

Figure 6.4   Single-wing formation.

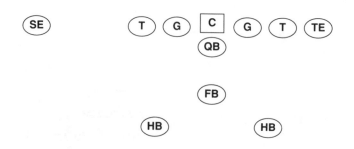

Figure 6.5   Wishbone formation.

Some coaches prefer to line up their teams in a three-back set, moving the flanker to a wingback (see Figure 6.4) or second halfback position to form a wishbone alignment (see Figure 6.5). The single-wing and wishbone formations are typically used by coaches who want their teams to run the ball much more than pass it.

Defensive Positions

Now it's time to look at the players you'll be asking to stop the opposing team from moving the football. Here are the basic defensive positions, with a short discussion of the skills and duties of each one.

Defensive Linemen

Youth football coaches put four to six players up front, on the line. The four-man front consists of two tackles and two ends. The five-man front adds a nose guard in the middle; the six-man front adds two ends who start in an upright position, much like outside linebackers (see next section).

Defensive tackles and defensive ends are primarily responsible for finding out who has the football and tackling that ballcarrier before he can gain yardage. It is also their duty to rush the passer when the offense attempts to throw the ball. To carry out their assignments, it is very helpful for defensive linemen to have adequate size and strength as well as great quickness to fend off or avoid blocks by offensive players.

Linebackers

Depending on the number of linemen used, you will want two to four linebackers on defense at all times. No matter how many you use, each should have a "nose" for the ball—that is, he should be able to read the offense's play and stop it quickly.

The standard three-linebacker set shown in Figure 6.6 complements the four-man front very nicely. In this alignment, you have a middle linebacker, who is the heart of the defense, and two outside linebackers.

The middle linebacker should be one of your best athletes and surest tacklers. The outside linebacker on the tight end side, often called *SAM* for short to indicate that he plays on the offense's *strong side*, must be strong enough to fend off blocks, but also fast enough to cover the tight end on pass routes. *WILL*, or the weakside linebacker,

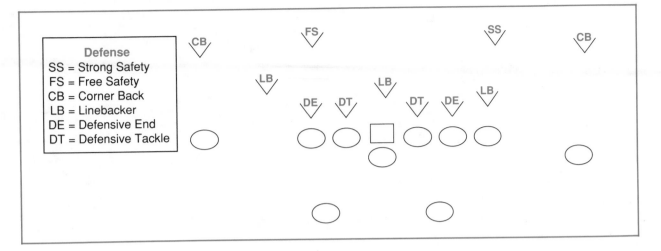

Figure 6.6 Defensive team alignment.

must be able to stand his ground against blocks by linemen and backs to prevent the offense from running the ball successfully.

Defensive Backs

The players responsible for preventing long runs and completed passes by the offense are called defensive backs. Again, depending on the alignment of your defensive front, the offense's set, and the game situation, you'll have three to five defensive backs in the game. Safeties have run and pass responsibilities. Cornerbacks cover the wide-outs.

All of these players must be agile and fast to cover speedy receivers. In addition, the safeties in particular must be good tacklers to assist linebackers in stopping the run.

Special Teams Positions

In addition to the basic offensive and defensive spots, you'll also need to designate players for special teams positions. Here is a very quick look at the key positions on each unit.

Punt and Kick Teams

Long snapper: Center on field goal and punt teams

Holder: Player who receives snap on field goal attempts and places the ball on the tee for the kicker

Kicker: Kicker on kickoff, field goal, and PAT teams (see Figure 6.7)

Punter: Kicker on punt team

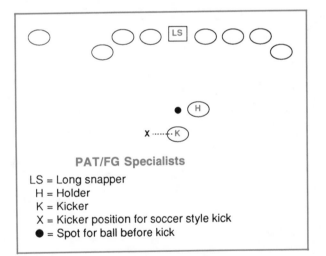

Figure 6.7 Alignment for PAT or field goal.

Punt and Kickoff Return Teams

Kick returner: Player furthest from kicker, whom the kickoff return team most wants to field and run with the ball

Punt returner: Player furthest from punter, whom the punt return team most wants to field and run with the ball

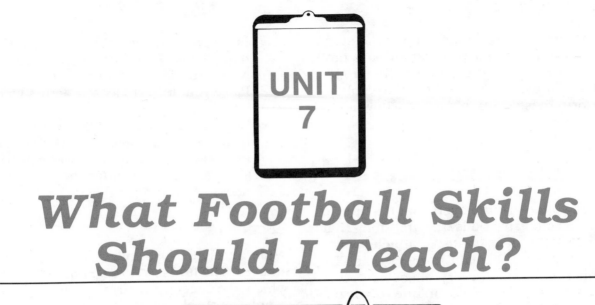

UNIT 7

What Football Skills Should I Teach?

To participate successfully in football, a player must be able to get in the proper stance, block, and tackle. This unit describes how you can teach these techniques. It also explains skills specific to various positions and outlines selected drills to help players develop them.

It is very important that you understand the skills of football and teach them properly. To improve their level of play and success, players must execute the skills of the game properly. Start out by teaching the very basics of any skill and then progress only when the players are able to perform that skill. Most football skills are not natural actions, so it is very important that you continue to review the basics with your players everytime you practice. If your players are not successful in performing a technique, you can probably trace it back to difficulty with one of the basic skills. For example, if your offensive lineman is getting beaten on his pass protection, he is probably standing too erect. You need to practice with him the basic stance, the initial step, and the proper body position for pass protection. Teams that are taught the proper skills and techniques and then are able to perform these skills in a game will win the most contests.

OFFENSIVE SKILLS

When you tell your players that it's time to work on offensive skills, the first thing that will pop into their minds is "touchdown." So you have to explain to them that TDs happen only when every offensive player properly executes the techniques of his position within the team's strategy. In this section, you'll learn how to instruct your players in these important, basic offensive skills.

Stance

The stance is the proper alignment of a player's body to start each play. Following is a description of the stances you should teach players at each position.

Offensive Linemen

Before the snap, offensive linemen should be positioned in a three-point stance. Figure 7.1 illustrates how this stance should look. Use these points to teach the correct stance to tackles, guards, and centers:

✔ Place the feet shoulder-width apart, in a heel-instep relationship, with the dominant foot back.

Figure 7.1 Proper three-point stance for an offensive lineman.

✔ Put very little weight on the down hand to allow for quick forward, backward, and lateral movement.
✔ Place your left arm loosely across your left thigh.
✔ Keep your back straight, with your head up to see defenders across the line of scrimmage. This position is the strongest and safest for the back and neck.

Receivers

Wide receivers use two basic types of stances. The first is a three-point stance, in which the receiver distributes his weight evenly, with his head up and his eyes focused either directly downfield or on the football (see Figure 7.2). His feet are staggered, which allows for a good explosion from the line of scrimmage. The second stance used by the wide receiver is a two-point or upright stance (see Figure 7.3). Its advantages are that the receiver can get off the line of scrimmage without being held up, and that he is in immediate position to receive quick passes.

Three-Point Stance

✔ Place the feet shoulder-width apart, in a heel-toe relationship, with the foot closest to the football staggered in a comfortable sprinter's position.
✔ Point knees and toes straight ahead.
✔ Keep your back straight, parallel to the ground, and your head up.

Figure 7.2 Three-point stance for wide receivers.

Two-Point Stance

✔ Place the feet shoulder-width apart, in a heel-toe relationship, with the foot closest to the football back slightly more than the other.

- ✔ Bend knees in a comfortable position.
- ✔ Keep weight on the balls of your feet.
- ✔ Keep your back straight, leaning forward slightly.
- ✔ Square your shoulders to the line of scrimmage.
- ✔ Hold your arms in a comfortable position.

Figure 7.3 Two-point stance for wide receivers.

Quarterback

A quarterback's stance must be poised and relaxed, reflecting confidence. The quarterback's feet should be comfortably spread,

Figure 7.4 The quarterback's stance from the front and the side.

approximately shoulder-width apart, and as close to the center's feet as possible. His knees should be slightly bent, and he should drop his hips while remaining as tall over the center as possible. The quarterback's shoulders should be parallel to the line of scrimmage, his head up to check the positioning of the defense (see Figure 7.4).

Running Backs

The most common stance for halfbacks and fullbacks is a two-point stance (see Figure 7.5). Players at these positions need to accelerate quickly from their backfield spot. Teach them to use the following stance before the ball is snapped:

- ✔ Place your feet about shoulder-width apart with your weight on the balls of your feet.
- ✔ Keep your feet near parallel for a quick burst in any direction.
- ✔ Bend you knees slightly with your hands on your knees.
- ✔ Keep your head up with eyes looking ahead.

Figure 7.5 Two-point stance for the running back.

If your running backs are going to use the three-point stance, teach them the same stance technique you taught the offensive lineman.

Stance Drills

Name. **Ready Stance Drill**

Purpose. To teach proper stance.

Organization. Players line up, each in the proper stance for his position. You inspect each player's stance, making necessary corrections. Then the players fire out for 5 yards and properly execute a designated skill from the stance. Be very aware of body position as the players come out of their stances.

Coaching Points. This drill will help you increase players' efficiency through learning their correct stance and developing good initial movement. Young players have a tendency to rush right into performing the skill, so stress the importance of a proper setup and quick first step.

Blocking

Blocking is the cornerstone of all successful offensive teams. Teams use blocking to move a defensive man out of the area where they want to run the football and to keep defensive linemen from tackling the quarterback.

Offensive linemen are involved in some type of blocking on every play. Running backs block when they are not carrying the football, and wide receivers block when they are not catching the football. Teach your players three types of blocks: the drive block, the downfield block, and the pass protection block.

Drive Block

The drive block is a one-on-one block used most often when a defensive lineman is lined directly over an offensive man, and the defensive man must be moved for the play to succeed. When teaching your players the drive block, emphasize these points (see Figure 7.6):

- ✔ Explode from your stance with the foot closest to the opponent and drive your hips forward on the third and fourth steps, through the block.

- ✔ Start with short, choppy steps, and keep your feet moving.
- ✔ Deliver the block from a wide base, and keep your head up and shoulders square.
- ✔ Punch hands or forearms into the opponent to establish momentum, and deliver the blow on impact with the forearms, not the head.
- ✔ Keep your head on the side of the opponent toward the hole, and follow through with short, choppy steps, turning the opponent away from the hole.

Figure 7.6 Proper blocking position.

Downfield Block

Teach your players two kinds of downfield blocks. A blocker should use the run-block technique when the ballcarrier is directly behind him. In this situation, he blocks the defender at full or three-quarter speed by attacking aggressively with the forearms and shoulders.

The cross-body block is another common and effective block to teach your players. This block may be used from in front of the defender or from an angle to his side. To make this block, a player must throw one arm in front of the defender's head. This motion causes the defender to move his head back and expose his body. As part of the same movement, the blocker whips his body laterally and makes contact at the defender's midsection. The blocker then rolls his body into the defender to complete the block. Remind players to never cross-body block a defender below the waist when outside the zone of 4 yards on either side of the center and 3 yards on either side of the line of scrimmage.

Pass Protection Block

The pass protection block keeps the defender from getting to the quarterback before he can throw the football. Teach your running backs and your offensive linemen the same techique for protecting the quarterback. Use the following sequential method to teach the pass protection block.

Initial Move and Setup

The initial move and setup technique is extremely important in pass blocking. The lineman must set up quickly, stepping with his inside foot first. The offensive lineman pushes up into a two-point stance with his down hand. The movement projects the offensive lineman into a position with his head up, eyes open wide, back straight, rear end down, hand and arms up, and feet positioned to move back or laterally in a split second. The depth behind the line of scrimmage should vary with the pass action called and the opponent's defensive front alignment.

Body Position

- ✔ Keep your head up and your rear end down.
- ✔ Keep your back straight.
- ✔ Place your feet shoulder-width apart, keep them moving, and flex your knees.
- ✔ Keep the weight of your body and head over your feet, never in front of them.
- ✔ Hold your elbows in with the hands, ready to ward off the challenge of the defensive lineman.

The lineman must position himself between the quarterback and the defensive pass rusher. He can do this by backing off

the line of scrimmage quickly after the snap. Instruct your offensive linemen that they should never get beat to their inside.

Punch

Delivering a blow to stop the charge of the defensive lineman takes good timing. The player must let the defensive lineman get as close as 6 inches and then deliver the blow to stop the charge. The lineman must strive to deliver a blow, step back away from the defensive lineman, and recoil. The player must deliver the punch with the elbows in close to the rib cage, locking the elbows and rolling the wrists to get power. No, we aren't recommending that you teach your linemen to throw left hooks at charging defenders. The linemen's hands and arms must stay within the planes of the shoulders (see Figure 7.7).

Figure 7.7 Proper position for pass protection.

Patience

Patience may be the hardest thing to teach an offensive lineman, because he must be the protector and not the aggressor. He must keep his legs under him and always remain in a good blocking position even after delivering the punch. An effective coaching point is to instruct linemen to keep their rear ends down and their knees bent at all times.

Footwork

The most important skill for an offensive lineman is the ability to move his feet. The correct foot movement is a shuffle, with the player keeping one foot in contact with the ground at all times. The linemen should never cross their feet and should keep their bodies parallel to the line of scrimmage with their backs to the quarterback at all times. The feet should be kept shoulder-width apart. Figure 7.7 shows the proper position for pass protection.

Pass Protection Drills

Name. **Quick Set Drill**

Purpose. To get linemen from their stance to a hitting position as quickly as possible.

Organization. The linemen line up in a circle in a good stance. On your command, they pop up into a correct pass protection position—taking a quick step with the inside foot, putting hands up in a punch position, and assuming a squat position, ready to strike a blow. To vary this drill, have them do this continuously for a minute—up, down, up, down.

Coaching Point. To increase effort and avoid monotony, make the drill competitive. Call out quarterback signals and identify the lineman who is quickest to get into the blocking position on the snap count.

Name. **Balance Drill**

Purpose. To help the linemen keep their feet apart and keep their bodies from being pushed, pulled, or tipped from side to side.

Organization. The players line up across from each other and grab the shoulder pads of the player opposite them. On your command, one of the partners, the defensive player, tries to get his opponent off balance by pushing, pulling, and tipping him from side to side. This forces the offensive player to get low, get a wide base, and move his feet to keep his balance. Switch partners and have players perform the drill again.

Coaching Points. Correct errors in technique such as not establishing a solid base and overextending the arms. Encourage defensive players to vary their attack and be active.

Name. **Punch Drill**

Purpose. To reinforce how players are to deliver a blow properly.

Organization. Use a punch board, a seven-man sled, blocking dummies, or teammates. Players should start in an upright position and deliver the blow as they would against a defensive lineman—aim for the armpits, elbows in, squat position. Players should then extend the arms, locking the elbows and rolling the wrists to give extra power. Players then shuffle step to the next bag and repeat the technique.

Coaching Points. Observe and correct players to make sure each punch is performed properly. Look for quick recovery and foot movement between blocks.

Name. **One-on-One Pass Protection**

Purpose. To put all the blocking techniques together in a live situation.

Organization. Each offensive lineman faces a defensive lineman on the line of scrimmage. The quarterback calls the cadence, and on the snap of the football the offensive lineman sets up in a pass protection position and tries to prevent the defensive lineman from pressuring the quarterback.

Coaching Points. Keep the number of offensive and defensive players down to three on a side. This will allow you to detect and correct mistakes to help the linemen improve. As players' skills progress, have the quarterback roll out to one side or the other, requiring the offensive linemen to protect a moving pocket.

Running the Football

Getting the Handoff

Instruct the running back that when he is getting the handoff from the quarterback, the elbow of his inside arm (the arm closest to the quarterback) should be up to receive the ball. The inside arm should be bent at the elbow (90-degree angle) and parallel to the ground at about shoulder level. The outside arm (the arm furthest from the quarterback) should be placed across the belt with the elbow close to the body, the palm of the hand turned up, and the fingers spread. Figure 7.8 shows a running back in proper handoff position. Allow your quarterback to place the football into the pocket formed by the running back.

Figure 7.8 The running back in proper handoff position.

Carrying the Football

After receiving the ball, the running back must protect the ball as much as possible. Teach the ballcarrier to immediately tuck the end of the ball under his arm and cover the front point of the ball with his hand. The ball should be carried away from the pressure of the defense; that is, when the ballcarrier is running to the right, the ball should be in his right arm with his hand over the point, and when he's running to the left, the ball should be in his left arm with his hand over the point. A coaching point is to carry the ball in the arm away from the inside linebacker.

Using Blockers

Coach your running backs to run toward the hole that has been called unless they see that the hole is closed. They should then head upfield to gain what yardage they can.

Teach them to run with a forward lean. This helps them to stay low and have a good forward drive.

Instruct the backs to make their cut at the last moment. They should approach the line of scrimmage with their shoulders square to the line. To prevent the defender from getting a solid tackle, a good running back will fake him by taking a step away from the defender, then cut back close to him as if he were cutting right through him. Coach each running back to set up his blockers by run-ning on the blocker's outside hip, and then, at the last moment, cut inside as the blocker takes out the defender.

Running Back Drill

Name. **Bag Drill**

Purpose. To teach players how to receive a proper handoff and keep the head up to make the correct read and cut.

Organization. This drill involves the center, the quarterback, and the running backs. The quarterback takes the snap from the center and hands the football to the running back (check for proper handoff position of the arms). The back has his eyes upfield running toward a dummy (representing a defender) held 3 yards away by the coach (see Figure 7.9). As the back approaches the dummy, the coach will move it to the right or the left, indicating that the back should cut in the opposite direction. This should be done at full speed to simulate game conditions. This helps players work on proper handoffs, hand placement on the football, and change of direction for the running backs.

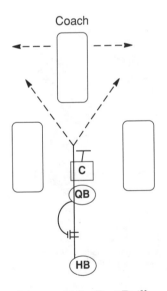

Figure 7.9 Bag Drill.

Coaching Points. Emphasize quick and clean execution of the handoff. Watch runners to see that they plant and push off the foot that is on the side to which you point the bag. And emphasize to your players that defenders will recover unless the runner bursts at full speed in the opposite direction.

Playing Quarterback

Taking the Snap

The quarterback's hands should be positioned so his top hand, or pressure hand, is pushing up on the center's rear end. This pressure tells the center where to snap the football. The bottom hand, or catch hand, should be positioned so the thumbs are together and the fingers extended, giving the center a good target to get the ball in. The quarterback's elbows should be slightly bent so he can allow for the center firing out on the snap.

The center should snap the ball slowly to the quarterback to make sure he is getting it properly and that the laces are placed at or near the fingers of the throwing hand. The snap should then be practiced at full speed. Spend five minutes each day on center-quarterback exchanges. Figure 7.10 illustrates a quarterback receiving the snap.

Figure 7.10   The quarterback receiving the snap.

The quarterback looks downfield, and when he receives the snap, he turns his head to see where he will hand off the ball. When he locates the target, he should keep his eyes on that player. On passing plays, he brings the football into his body at the belt and then raises it up to the armpit in a ready-to-throw position. The quarterback should not swing the football.

Footwork

The quarterback's initial "pushoff" begins when he receives the ball, never before. A transfer of weight must precede the pushoff; from a balanced position, the quarterback shifts his weight to the stable or away foot. His lead foot steps in the direction of the play in a swinging motion and must be kept close to the ground.

Handoff

The quarterback is completely responsible for the success or failure of the handoff. He must adjust to the running back's path and speed and get him the football.

Instruct the quarterback to keep both hands on the ball as long as possible and to lock the football into the pocket that the running back provides. Have him try to make the exchange with the foot on the same side as the give hand nearest the running back. Although not tremendously important, this allows for greater reach and balance. Coach your quarterback to place or press the ball firmly into the ballcarrier's pocket, allowing his give hand to ride the ball into place.

Dropback

After receiving the ball from the center, the quarterback usually takes either three, five, or seven steps back, depending on the length of the receiver route. There are three different types of drops—the crossover, the backpedal, and the rollout. The crossover involves bending the knees and lowering the rear end to begin movement and gain momentum. This first step (to the right for right-handed quarterbacks) should be parallel to the line of scrimmage, followed by several crossover steps to the setting point (see Figure 7.11). In the last two steps before anchoring, the quarterback should shift his weight forward to slow up and should prepare to position his feet for the throw.

The backpedal begins with the same body position used in the crossover. However, the first step (with the right foot for right-handed quarterbacks) is directly backward, followed by a sequence of backpedals. Three-, five-, and seven-step drops are most common, allowing the quarterback to plant for the throw. Throughout the drop, the quarterback should keep his shoulders parallel to the line of scrimmage.

The rollout is a general term for any drop that involves the quarterback moving laterally to the line of scrimmage. The popular sprintout technique consists of the quarterback simply sprinting to a designated spot to one side of the field several yards behind the line of scrimmage. The bootleg is another rollout option, where the quarterback fakes a handoff to a back on one side of the field, then sprints in the opposite direction.

The crossover is the quickest and most conventional drop. The backpedal is slower but gives the quarterback more time to spot receivers and read the defense. The rollout is best for quick quarterbacks who can run the football and short quarterbacks who have trouble seeing downfield over tall linemen.

Figure 7.11 Quarterback in a crossover drop.

Throwing the Football

The quarterback keeps the ball in the ready position at the armpit before raising it straight up to throw. His elbow extends out and leads the ball toward the throw. He should grip the ball with the fingers over the laces and the index finger close to the tip of the football to guide it. There should be some space between the quarterback's palm and

the football. He releases the ball with the thumb and the wrist facing down. On release, the index finger should be last to leave the football and should be pointed directly toward the target. Figure 7.12 shows the quarterback in proper throwing position.

Figure 7.12 The quarterback in proper throwing position.

Quarterback Drills

Name. **Dropback**

Purpose. To teach the quarterback to get into proper throwing position as quickly as possible.

Organization. The quarterback takes the snap from the center and practices three-, five-, and seven-step drops.

Coaching Points. Have the quarterbacks work on the crossover, backpedal, and rollout drops. Watch for proper footwork, ball carrying position, and setup.

Name. **Set, Pick, and Fire**

Purpose. To improve the quarterback's reaction upon setup.

Organization. The quarterback takes a quick drop and sets to deliver the football. Three or four other players are stationed downfield, facing him in a horizontal line spread evenly across the football field. Each of these players has an assigned number.

The coach calls out one of the numbers. After the quarterback has set his feet, he must quickly reset them in the direction of the designated player and deliver the football to him, utilizing the proper throwing mechanics.

Coaching Points. Use an equal number of same-direction and opposite-direction receivers. This will develop quarterbacks' ability to throw to the primary and secondary receivers. Watch that upon reset the quarterback gets a solid plant with the back foot.

Receiving

Running Patterns

When the play is called in the huddle, the receiver is told what pattern to run. This pattern is selected from many options on a pass tree (see Figure 7.13). Pass patterns 1, 2, and 3 are reserved for the running backs.

The most important thing you should teach a receiver is to *explode* off the line of scrimmage. He should run to the outside shoulder of the defensive back, forcing the defender to turn his shoulders parallel to the line of scrimmage to cover him. Next, the receiver must come under control at the *breaking point* of this pattern. He then plants his foot, turns his head and shoulders, and reacts to the football.

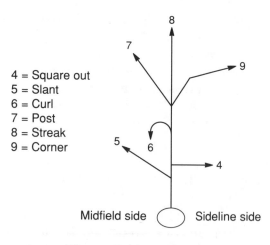

4 = Square out
5 = Slant
6 = Curl
7 = Post
8 = Streak
9 = Corner

Figure 7.13 Pass tree.

Catching the Football

The next step in coaching receivers is to teach them how to catch the football. This is a matter of concentration and dedication. The receiver should watch the football into his hands. If the football is thrown high, the receiver should catch it with thumbs together; if it is thrown low, the receiver should catch it with little fingers together. Also, it is important that you teach the receiver to catch the football in his hands and not trap it against his body.

In practices, give receivers the opportunity to catch every type of pass that they will see in games. As a coach, you cannot expect athletes to perform things in a game that you have not worked on in practice. Instruct receivers to tuck the ball under the arm and protect it after making the catch. Success will help the receivers gain confidence, and touchdowns reinforce that catching the ball is fun.

Receiver Drills

Name. **Turn Drill**

Purpose. To force the receiver to get into a position to see the ball and to concentrate on catching it.

Organization. Two lines of receivers are on each side of the field, with a quarterback throwing to each line. The receiver in each line has his back to the quarterback. The quarterback yells "go" as he passes the ball to the first receiver in line. On the command, the receiver must snap his head quickly around, locate and catch the ball, tuck it in, and turn upfield with it. Have receivers alternate turning the head over each shoulder.

Coaching Points. Work on short, lofted throws initially, with receivers going at three-quarter speed. Increase the speed and length of pass routes as receivers improve.

Name. **Concentration Drill**

Purpose. To get receivers to focus on the ball and watch it all the way into their hands, even when they know they're going to get hit.

Organization. You'll need several footballs with 1-inch numbers painted on each panel, and three hand-held blocking shields. Three people holding the hand shields line up 3 yards apart, forming an equilateral triangle. Have a receiver run into the middle of the triangle. As the receiver enters it, the quarterback should throw him a high pass. The

Figure 7.14 Concentration Drill.

receiver must jump to catch the pass. As soon as his hands touch the ball, the three players holding shields should jam the receiver with their shields. The receiver must call out the number painted on the ball and hold onto the pass. Figure 7.14 illustrates the Concentration Drill.

Coaching Points. Keep score to determine how many catches and correct numbers receivers have at the end of the drill. Track their improvement throughout the season.

Kicking Game

The kicking game is a very important part of football. About one-fourth of the game involves kicking, so you definitely need to spend time on it. Three phases of the kicking game that we address in this chapter are the punt, the place kick, and the kickoff.

The Punt

The punt is used on fourth down to turn the ball over to the opponent. The punting team's objective is to give the opponent a less favorable field position. Coach your kickers to follow these guidelines to punt successfully.

- The punter lines up 10 yards behind the center.
- Assume a comfortable stance with knees slightly bent and arms extended.
- When you drop the ball, there should be no movement at the elbows, wrists, or shoulders.
- Drop the ball perfectly parallel to the ground with the tip turned slightly in.
- Your foot speed is not as important as making proper contact on the center of the ball.
- The non-kicking leg should remain in contact with the ground.
- Allow the kicking leg to extend and follow through after the kick (see Figure 7.15).

The key to coaching a punter is to teach him correct techniques and then allow him to practice and develop his own rhythm. He should strive for consistency in height and distance.

Figure 7.15 Proper kicking technique for punter.

Punt coverage involves organizing your punt team in such a way that they can protect the punter, cover the punt, and tackle the ballcarrier before he can advance the ball upfield. The ball should be kicked for distance, and it also should remain in the air long enough to give the coverage team enough time to get downfield and make the tackle. Figure 7.16 shows a common punt coverage team alignment.

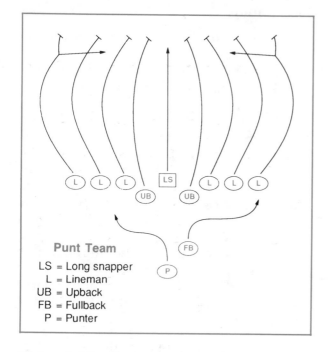

Figure 7.16   Alignment and coverage of punting teams.

The Place Kick

There are two basic types of place kicking—the straight-ahead style (see Figure 7.17) and the soccer style (see Figure 7.18). Both are effective. Have your kickers follow these coaching points, regardless of the kicking style they use.

- ✔ Emphasize accuracy on every kick.
- ✔ Avoid overpowering the ball; keep a good timing and rhythm going.
- ✔ Make proper contact with the ball.
- ✔ Plant the foot in the same way on each kick.
- ✔ The foot must hit the ball squarely each time.
- ✔ Proper body alignment is necessary on each kick.

Give kickers the opportunity to practice kicking in gamelike situations.

Figure 7.17   Straight-ahead style of place kicking.

Figure 7.18   Soccer style of place kicking.

The Kickoff

The main difference between the kickoff and the place kick involves the approach phase of the kick. A longer approach run is used on the kickoff, allowing the kicker to build up more speed and momentum before the kick.

The kicker lines up 5 to 10 yards from the football. As he approaches the ball, he must

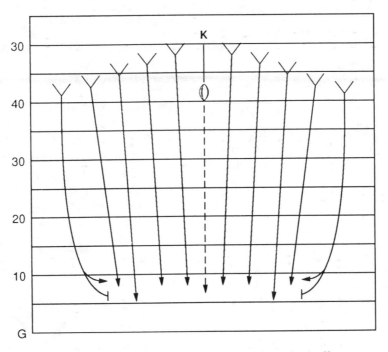

Figure 7.19   Proper coverage for a kickoff.

adjust his steps so that he runs through the ball without slowing. The key coaching point on the kickoff is for the kicker to make contact with the ball and work on being consistent. Figure 7.19 shows proper coverage for a kickoff.

Spend time daily working to improve some phase of your team's kicking game.

DEFENSIVE SKILLS

Playing defense is part instinct, part effort, and part technique. You can't do much about your players' instinct; most young players love the game, so effort isn't a problem; the key for any football coach is to teach and develop players' defensive skills. The rest of this unit will tell you how.

Stance

The proper initial alignment of the body for the defensive player is very important. Coach the defensive linemen, linebackers, and defensive backs about the proper stances for their respective positions.

Defensive Linemen

The typical stance for defensive linemen is similar to the offensive lineman's three-point stance (refer to Figure 7.1). However, some defensive linemen are more comfortable with the outside hand down on the ground, creating a four-point stance as shown in Figure 7.20. Give your players the following pointers:

✔ Placing more weight on the hands enables you to move forward.

Figure 7.20   Defensive lineman in a four-point stance.

✔ A stance that is a little wider allows for better balance when you're being blocked.

✔ Keep your outside hand (away from the blocker) free to try pass rush techniques and to keep from getting hooked.

✔ Keep your body low to the ground, and control the line of scrimmage from underneath the opponent's shoulder pads.

Linebackers

The linebacker should have a good balanced stance, which means that his feet are shoulder-width apart and slightly staggered. Figure 7.21 shows the proper stance for a linebacker. Teach your linebackers the following points:

✔ Bend your knees slightly to insure low body position.

✔ Poise the arms in front of the body as you get ready to take on a blocker.

✔ Focus your eyes on the man you are to get the key from.

✔ One foot is slightly forward; step with this foot first as you react to the key and find the football.

Figure 7.21   Proper stance for a linebacker.

Defensive Backs

Coach the defensive backs to line up with a slightly staggered stance in a relaxed position. Instruct your players as follows:

✔ Keep your feet slightly staggered, with the outside foot back.

✔ Point the toes straight ahead.

✔ Focus eyes on the man you are to key.

✔ Assume a slightly crouching position with your knees bent a little.

✔ Take a short read step on the snap, and then react to the play. Figure 7.22 shows the proper stance for a defensive back.

Figure 7.22   Proper stance for a defensive back.

Stance Drills

Name. **Winning From the Start**

Purpose. To teach defensive players the proper presnap position and initial movement.

Organization. Have your players line up according to their position—defensive linemen, linebackers, and defensive backs—and instruct them to get into their proper stances. Then visually inspect the stances using the guidelines presented in this section to make sure they are correct. Next, have each player move out of his stance quickly to perform his responsibility, so that on the snap count, the defensive linemen step forward, the defensive backs go backward, and the linebackers go either forward, lateral, or backward. Watch to make sure players do not take false steps and that they maintain a good hitting position throughout their movement.

Coaching Points. Vary quick and long counts to keep players from anticipating the snap. Also have them hurry back into position each time and try different positions during the drill.

Tackling

If you want to have a good defensive team, you must teach your defensive players to tackle. Players who are just beginning to learn the game may only be able to get into a position to grab the runner and pull him down, but as the players grow and progress, it is important that you teach them the proper techniques of tackling.

The tackler should always be in the proper hitting position and be given a target to focus on in making the tackle (this is usually the area of the runner's belt buckle). As he focuses on this target, his opponent will not be able to fake him out with a fancy shoulder move. The three basic tackles that your players will be using are the head-on tackle, the angle tackle, and the open-field tackle. Here are some coaching points for each type.

Head-On Tackle

The head-on tackle is used when the tackler is lined up straight across from the offensive runner, who is coming toward him. The tackler should first make sure he is in a good hitting position and is ready to make the tackle. Emphasize the following points to your tacklers:

✔ Make sure that you are under control so as not to overrun the ballcarrier or dive and miss the tackle.

✔ Maintain a wide, balanced stance; keep the feet moving with choppy steps.
✔ Extend your arms and head in front of your body.
✔ Keep your head up, your back arched, and your knees slightly bent.
✔ Slide your head to the outside just before making contact.
✔ Your shoulder drives into the runner's stomach region as your hips are thrust through.
✔ With your arms, grasp behind the legs of the ballcarrier and pull him toward you.
✔ Lift and pull the ballcarrier toward you as you take him off his feet.

Figure 7.23 shows proper tackling technique. This is the ideal tackle technique to strive for in teaching your young athletes tackling skills.

Figure 7.23   Proper tackling technique.

The Angle Tackle

This tackle is necessary when the ballcarrier is running a wide play or gets close to the sideline. Coach your tacklers using these guidelines:

✔ Keep under control and be ready to move in any direction.

✔ It's important to maintain a good balanced stance in a good hitting position.

✔ Drive your head in front of the ballcarrier's number, across the line of his run.

✔ Drive your shoulder upward on the runner at about waist level.

✔ With your arms, grasp the runner behind the legs and lift him off the ground.

✔ Arch your back to lift and drive through the ballcarrier.

✔ Keep the feet moving with short choppy steps as you finish the tackle.

The Open-Field Tackle

This tackle is made after the runner has cleared the line of scrimmage or when a receiver has caught the football and the defensive man is the only player between the ballcarrier and the goal line. Coach the player that in the open field the most important thing to do is to get ahold of the opponent and pull him to the ground. Stress these coaching points:

✔ Keep under control with your legs bent.

✔ Use the sideline to your advantage, penning in or getting an angle on the runner.

✔ Your number-one priority is to grasp the runner.

✔ Once you have a hold on the runner, help should be soon to arrive. But, if possible, try to drive him out of bounds or pull him to the turf.

✔ Don't worry about driving through the man or delivering a hard blow. Your sole responsibility is to get ahold of the player and prevent the score.

Tackling Drills

Name. **Form Tackling Drill**

Purpose. To teach players the basic tackling techniques.

Organization. Form two lines of players with the leaders of each line facing each other. One will be the ballcarrier and the other the defensive player. The ballcarrier runs straight ahead at the defensive player, and the defensive player must first get into a position to tackle the ballcarrier and then make the tackle. The next players in line then continue the drill, and so on.

Coaching Points. Have players walk through the drill to start, and then as their technique improves, gradually increase the speed and intensity of the drill. Stand near and to the side of the point of contact and make corrections according to the techniques described in the tackling section.

Name. **Sideline Tackling**

Purpose. To teach the players to use the sideline to their advantage and judge the angle to make the tackle.

Organization. The ballcarrier lines up behind the quarterback on the hash mark, takes the pitch, and runs a sweep toward the sideline. The defensive player is 5 yards in front of the center, and he runs on an angle to intersect the ballcarrier before he can get outside and down the sideline. The defensive man should execute the angle tackle as described in the tackling section (see Figure 7.24).

Coaching Points. Match up players of similar size and speed. Give defenders enough

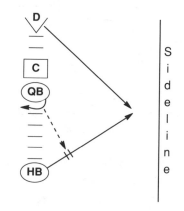

Figure 7.24 Sideline tackling drill.

repetitions that they become proficient at making this tackle.

Rushing the Passer

The following techniques are for the defensive linemen to rush the passer.

Bull Rush

A bull rush occurs when the defensive man gets control of the offensive blocker by locking his arms in the offensive blocker's armpits, and with the leverage provided by locking his elbows he can lift the offensive lineman up, forcing him back into the quarterback. This type of rush requires good arm and hand strength.

Swim Technique

The defender employs this technique by driving hard for the blocker's outside shoulder, forcing him to square up and set himself for the rush (see Figure 7.25). When the blocker begins to square up and set, the defender brings his outside arm up and hits the opponent on the side of the shoulder in an attempt to knock him off balance. Next, the pass rusher brings his inside arm over

Figure 7.25　Swim technique.

the top of the blocker's outside shoulder in a swimming motion. Once the inside arm is over the blocker, the defender pushes off and moves toward the quarterback. Note that the swim motion and the pushoff must be one continuous movement.

Undercut Technique

With the undercut technique, the defender attacks the blocker low and hard. As he closes toward the offensive player, he executes a forearm blow with his inside arm to the blocker's inside shoulder. The purpose of this maneuver is to turn the blocker's shoulders toward the undercut side. As the blocker's shoulder turns, the defender steps inside with his outside foot and ducks under the blocker, continuing on to the quarterback. The player must coordinate the forearm shiver and undercut as one continuous movement.

Pass Rush Drills

Name. **Pass Rush Technique**

Purpose. To help the defensive linemen rush the passer.

Organization. Line your defensive lineman across an imaginary line of scrimmage facing an offensive lineman. Instruct the offensive lineman to set up in a pass protection position. Then instruct the defensive lineman to walk through the ball rush, swing and undercut techniques to get to the quarterback.

Coaching Points. Observe and make corrections, stopping the action whenever necessary. When players have mastered the basic techniques, have them progress to a one-on-one drill against the offensive line to see how well they employ the techniques in a game-like situation.

Covering Receivers

The defense must be able to cover the receivers to stop the offense from moving the ball through the air. Spend time training your players to defend the pass. Following are some of the necessary skills.

Proper Alignment

The defensive corners should line up 5 to 7 yards off the wide receivers. The safety should line up 8 to 12 yards deep off the tight end or in the middle of the field if you are playing only one safety.

Backpedal

Instruct your players to bend at the waist with a forward body lean. The backpedal should start with a step backward with the back foot and a push off the front foot. As the player backpedals he should reach back with each step and pull his body over his feet. His arms should move in a normal, relaxed running fashion. The player should be under control so that when the receiver makes his break to catch the ball, the defensive man is ready to drive on him.

Pass Coverage

The basic coverage is man-to-man. This means that a defensive player is assigned to each offensive receiver wherever he goes. An example of man-to-man coverage is shown in Figure 7.26. Use the following guidelines in teaching your players how to cover receivers.

- ✔ Keep your eyes focused primarily on the receiver you are covering (at his belt region).
- ✔ Maintain a 3- to 4-yard cushion between you and the receiver.
- ✔ Never turn your back on the receiver.
- ✔ Once the ball is in the air, play the ball aggressively.

Covering Receiver Drills

Name. **Backpedal Drill**

Purpose. To teach and let players practice the proper fundamentals of executing the backpedal.

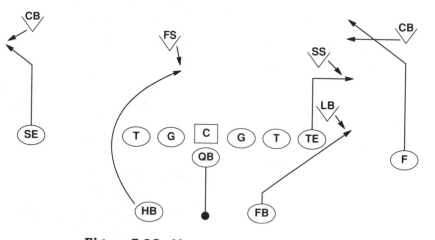

Figure 7.26 Man-to-man pass coverage.

Organization. The defensive player faces the coach. As you raise the ball, he begins his backpedal. After he has backpedaled about 10 yards, throw a catchable pass to the right or left of the defensive man.

Coaching Points. Make sure that the defensive man follows the techniques discussed in the section on covering receivers. Specifically, emphasize that defenders must drive toward the football as soon as they see its direction and flight.

Name. **Square Drill**

Purpose. To help players develop the ability to break squarely from a backpedal.

Organization. The defensive player aligns near the hash mark. As you raise the ball, the defender backpedals for 5 to 7 yards, and you move the ball to the player's right. The player turns and breaks squarely to his right, sprinting hard 5 yards and then coast-ing 5 yards (see Figure 7.27). Two to four players can perform the drill in the same box.

Coaching Points. Watch for the player making a proper plant step when he changes direction; try to correct players who make false steps.

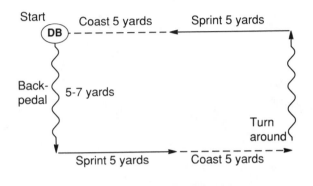

Figure 7.27 Square Drill.

UNIT 8

What Team Strategies Should I Use?

To be a successful coach, you must develop your own football coaching philosophy. We talked about your coaching outlook in Unit 2. But a football coaching philosophy is more specific to the sport—what you consider most important and what you emphasize to players in terms of teaching the Xs and Os.

After you've developed a philosophy, you'll need to establish strategies that your players can learn and implement in a game situation. You'll set offensive goals and decide what kind of offense you want to employ to move the football. You'll also set defensive goals and decide what defense you'll run. You must also determine your approach on special teams and the amount of time you'll spend to develop these skills.

Offensive Goals

The objectives you set must be realistic and important—not just to you, but to your players. If your team is incapable of, or not interested in achieving them, then the objectives serve little purpose.

Perhaps the most obvious objective of any offensive football team is to score. But scoring is an outcome based on the team's ability to

- execute consistently,
- move the football, and
- maintain possession.

Execute Consistently

To execute consistently, you must run the same plays throughout the season and work on their execution. Select a simple offense and teach it well. A few well-executed plays can give even the best opponents all they can handle. If your offense has too many plays, chances are your team, not your opponents, will be confused.

Consistent execution stems from your athletes understanding the plays and practicing them over and over. Every player must know what is expected of him for each running play. And practicing these plays against the defense that you expect opponents to play will help your players visualize the way each play is designed to be run. If your players know that a team goal is consistent execution, they'll be more eager to perform the plays as often as necessary to make them work in a game.

Approach your team's passing game in the same way. Teach your receivers the proper patterns to run, and your quarterback the proper depth to drop to throw the football. Your players need time to perform the pattern several times until they'll feel confident that it will work. You might run one pattern as many as 30 times in practice before you use it in an actual game.

Decide on a game plan early in the week, then simplify it so that on game day you have only five running plays, five pass patterns, and two goal line plays. You'll help your team execute consistently if you commit yourself to using a limited number of

plays each week and giving the players enough repetitions so that they eliminate mistakes.

Know the SCORE

Here is a good slogan that's positive and reminds you and your players that doing the basics well is the key to success

S— Simple as you can make it

C— Complete instructions for each player

O— One player executing poorly makes the whole team suffer

R— Repeat many times

E— Every player is involved

Move the Football

The object of offensive football is to move the football down the field and score, by either throwing the ball or running it. Running basic plays against the defense you anticipate seeing is the best way to prepare your team to move the football in a game.

The offensive team must believe they can march the football down the field regardless of the team they're playing or the defense they're facing. Use your play selection to expose a defense's weaknesses, and play to the strengths of your offense.

Maintain Possession

The offense should be aware that when they control the football, the opponent cannot score. To keep control, the offense must consistently produce first downs and keep the clock running. An effective running game combined with a good short passing game is hard to stop. Four yards a crack on running plays and high-percentage, 5- to 10-yard passes can keep the chains moving steadily toward the opponent's goal line.

Maintaining possession is especially important when your team has a narrow lead at the end of a game. The other team can't score if it doesn't get the ball.

Score

The touchdown is the primary objective and the field goal a secondary objective on an offensive drive. Passing may get you to the goal line faster, but a long march to the goal via the running game can take the heart out of the other team's defense. And there's nothing like a touchdown or a field goal to get your team fired up. Your team will be more excited and execute with more intensity if they experience the rewards of their efforts. Scoring gives the players confidence and reinforces the system you are using to coach.

Offensive Strategies

In many successful offenses, the coaches have developed an effective offensive system and have developed game plans incorporating this system into a strategy. The offensive system should have both a solid running game and an effective passing attack.

Running Game

You must consider certain elements in the development of a running game. The most important step is to design plays in which the blocking and the backfield action work together. The backfield action on any play must be designed to put the running back at the point of attack just as the hole is opening. Three types of blocks can help accomplish this: fast or quick blocking on straight-ahead plays, fold blocking on slower hitting plays, and power blocking on sweeps. Figure 8.1 shows examples of the three types of blocking.

You should also set up the running game so that it is effective and easy to communicate. The simplest way to communicate the running plays is to number each hole and back. Figure 8.2 shows how this is done. The running back runs the ball into the hole that is called. For example, the play "32" means that the number 3 back runs the ball through the number 2 hole.

In developing a running game it is important that you consider different series of

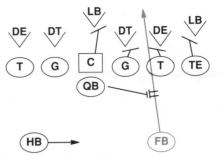

Straight man-for-man block

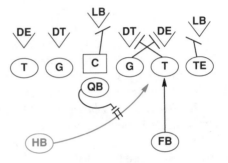

Fold blocking

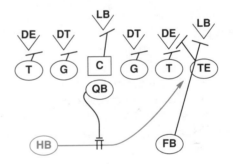

Power blocking (double team)

Figure 8.1 Three basic schemes for running plays.

plays that can all be successful. All series should include built-in dimension—that part of a given series that provides for variation of backfield movement. Dimension makes it difficult for the defense to determine the point of attack when the ball is snapped. This forces the defense to respect your entire attack. An example of a series is a DIVE 30 and a TRAP 30. These both involve the number 3 back running through the hole right in center of the line, but the back gets there by different actions and the blocking is different.

The running game should give you the opportunity to run the football in every offensive

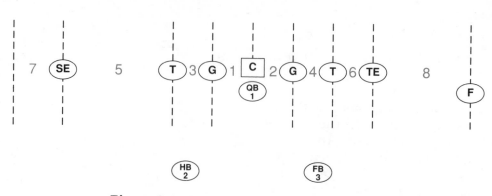

Figure 8.2 Hole and numbering of backs.

hole. By incorporating series of plays, you'll be able to run the various holes in more than one way. The game plan, however, should include only four or five running plays chosen from the total series of plays. These are the plays you will perfect for a chosen opponent.

The most successful football teams use runs that are most effective against the opponent they are playing. For example, if the defense is coming across the line of scrimmage very hard, you would use the trap series. With a rushing defense, it is easier for an offensive lineman to get an angle if a trap is called. Sometimes the defender will take himself out (overrun) the play; othertimes he can be blocked from the side. Against a reading defense, the dive and sweep would be effective. If the defense stacks the line of scrimmage, you may be better off throwing the ball.

The running backs are an integral part of a good running offense. Coach them to gain yardage on every play. They should be competitive and have the desire to be successful. A running back who is hard to tackle, who keeps his feet driving, and who at times is his own blocker will make you and your team winners.

Passing Game

The forward pass is an effective way to gain yardage offensively and also to score points. Several reasons for throwing the football include that it helps individual player development, forces the defense to defend the whole field, gains yardage on offense, and appeals to the crowd.

If you are going to pass the football, it is important that you do a good job of drilling the quarterbacks and receivers in the basic skills covered in Unit 7. Keep the passing attack very simple so that the quarterbacks and receivers know what to do. Timing is very important to the success of a passing attack, so you must allow time in practice for players to make many repetitions of the basic patterns.

The passing game starts with a pass tree (see Figure 7.13). These are patterns that the receivers run to get open to catch the football. The quarterback drops straight back (as described on pages 50-51) and throws the football to the open receiver.

Different pass patterns may be helpful in different situations. The curl pattern is used when the defensive man is retreating too fast. The receiver drives deep and then curls back to the football (see Figure 8.3a). The square out pattern is very successful when the defensive man is playing off the receiver (see Figure 8.3b). The receiver runs downfield 10 yards and then cuts sharply to the sideline, catching the ball just before he steps out of bounds. A crossing pattern is very effective against man-to-man coverage. Figure 8.3c shows two receivers crossing downfield. The defensive man is screened off on the crossing action, and one of the receivers usually comes open. The last pattern, the streak, is used if you have a receiver with speed and the defensive back is playing tight on the receiver. The receiver shows a curl move, then breaks to the outside and sprints down the sideline (see Figure 8.3d).

The passing game takes time to develop, and you must be patient to bring the separate

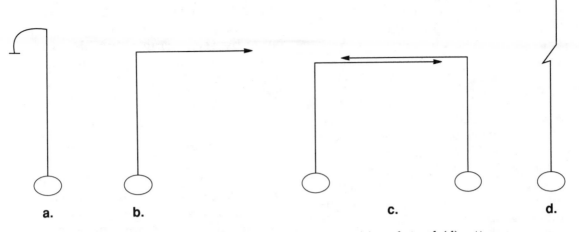

Figure 8.3 Curl (a), square out (b), crossing (c), and streak (d) patterns.

parts of this offense together. The next two drills should help.

Offensive Team Drills

Name. **Pass Skeleton**

Purpose. To develop the quarterback's passing skills and give the receivers a chance to run their patterns against a preparation defense.

Organization. The skeleton offensive group (quarterback, three receivers, and two running backs) line up on the line of scrimmage and run a pass pattern against the linebackers and defensive backs (Figure 8.4). The defense is told what defense to run, while the offensive group works on their pass play execution.

Coaching Points. Mix in some play action passes emphasizing good fakes by the quarterback and running backs. Encourage receivers to run crisp routes, using feints and bursts to elude the coverage. Also, try to determine what type and length of passes the quarterback can complete most consistently.

Name. **Team Offense**

Purpose. To run all of the offensive runs and passes against a defensive unit.

Organization. The plays that you are planning to run in the game are called in the huddle and then run against a team of defenders who react to the football but let the offense block them. The backs and receivers go at full speed.

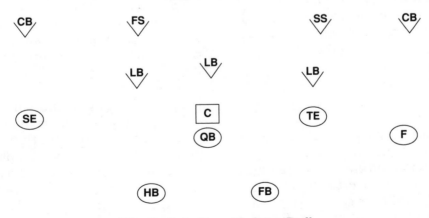

Figure 8.4 Pass Skeleton Drill.

Coaching Points. Look for offensive lineman to blow off the line of scrimmage and get a jump on the defense. Emphasize quickness and execution at the skill positions.

Defensive Goals

Every defense has a purpose. You can design your defense to either blitz, penetrate, pursue, contain, or perform any number of tactics to disrupt or stop the offense. Your defensive approach should reflect the talents of your players. Your basic defensive alignment must capitalize on their strengths and compensate for their weaknesses.

For example, if you have a somewhat big, slow team, use more linemen on the line of scrimmage and try to control and contain the offense. If you have a small, quick team, use more linebackers and do more blitzing to take advantage of their quickness. Once you have determined your style of defense, stay with it.

The three most important goals a defense can strive to accomplish are

- prevent the easy touchdown,
- get possession of the ball, and
- score.

Prevent the Easy Touchdown

Although the obvious objective of defensive football is to keep the opposition from scoring, a more functional objective of defensive play is to prevent the opposition from scoring the easy touchdown with a long pass or a long run. Make your opponent earn every point it scores by having a defense that challenges every yard. Praise players for preventing first downs and stopping the opponent's drives downfield.

Get Possession of the Football

The defensive team may gain possession of the ball by holding the opponent to fewer than 10 yards on four downs, forcing a punt, intercepting a pass, recovering a fumble or a blocked punt. Turnovers can also motivate a defense when it is having trouble stopping an opponent.

Score

The defense can score on a punt return or an intercepted pass, by advancing a blocked punt, by recovering a fumble in the end zone, by advancing any fumbled ball for a score, or by tackling the offensive player in their own end zone for a safety.

Defensive Strategies

You should have a plan for every situation your defense faces. In developing that plan, remember to include tactics that attack the offense and make things happen. In addition, your defensive scheme must have options designed to contain the offense in long yardage situations.

Attacking Defense

Use the following information to coach your defensive team to attack any running or passing game.

Alignments

If the offense is moving the ball, the defense must be able to make slight changes in alignment during the game to slow them down. For example, if the opponent is running the ball up the middle at your linebackers, switch to a defense that puts a defensive lineman in the middle.

Proper Keys

A defensive skill that is more important at advanced levels is the ability to "read" what the offense is going to do before the ball is snapped. The obvious advantage to doing this is that your defenders will be able to anticipate the play and stop it. If you try to teach your players how to read the offense, keep the reads few and simple.

The most basic read is made by "keying" on an opponent's formation, tendencies in play selection, or individual player cues. For example, a defensive back may key on the offensive tackle on his side of the field. If he sees the lineman set up to pass protect, he can assume it's a pass play and focus on covering his receiver. If the defensive back sees the lineman drive block, he can anticipate a running play and move into position to tackle the ballcarrier.

Flexibility

It is very important that you have a knowledge of football and learn as much as you can about your defense's strengths and weaknesses so you will be able to make the proper adjustments during the game. The coach must be fully prepared to cover various formations and series of plays that the defense may encounter. For example, if you are running a three-deep secondary and the offense is passing the ball, you may go to the four-deep secondary.

If the offense gives you an unusual formation, your defensive players must know how to adjust. The offense's position on the field, the score, the time left in the game, and the type of offense your team is facing are all factors that influence the defense that should be run.

As the coach, you might consider limiting the defense according to the skill level of your team. It is more effective to run a few defenses well than to run many defenses poorly.

The skills that we talked about in Unit 7 are good guidelines to incorporate into the total picture of a team defense. Team defense involves a group of players performing their individual techniques for the good of the team. Get the right players at the point of attack at the right time, and your team will be successful.

Defense Must Be Fun

Defensive football players are the aggressive kids who love to run and hit people. If you encourage emotion in defensive players, they will get excited when they make a tackle, recover a fumble, or intercept a pass. This excitement adds to team unity, and the players will perform at a higher level.

It is also important to encourage team tackling (where more than one person tackles the ballcarrier). This motivates defensive players to swarm to the ballcarrier and adds to team spirit. Stress hard work in an attempt to gain success, but make sure you add fun to the game.

Pressure Defense

The pressure defense is designed to force the offensive team into making mistakes. An example of this is when the defense forces the quarterback to throw the football before he is ready. Teach your defensive players the following points:

- A pressure defense uses a man-to-man pass coverage and tries to bump the receiver as he starts to run his pattern.
- The linebackers attack the line of scrimmage on the snap, trying to disrupt the offensive players' blocking schemes.
- The defensive alignment employs eight men who can rush within 5 yards of the line of scrimmage.
- The defensive players can jump up into the line of scrimmage and then retreat. They may loop on their pass rush. They may rush two players through the same defensive hole to confuse the offense.

The pressure defense is a good strategy to use if you have confidence in your players' abilities and techniques. This is important because in this defense your defensive backs are isolated one-on-one with their receivers with no help from the safety.

The pressure defense changes the tempo of the game, preventing the opponent from retaining possession of the football and driving down the field. The pressure defense is a good change-up; use it when the offense is not expecting it. If you find a blitz that gives the offense trouble or that they cannot pick up, keep using it until they make the proper adjustment. Figure 8.5 shows a sample alignment for a pressure defense.

Contain Defense

The contain defense plays a little softer than the pressure defense and tries to keep the offense from getting outside or getting deep. The defensive ends play for position to prevent ballcarriers from getting outside of them. After the defensive player reads his key, he first controls the gap or area of the field that he is responsible for, then reacts to the football. The defensive backs employ

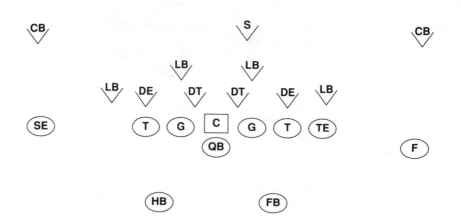

Figure 8.5 Alignment for a pressure defense.

a zone coverage on passes to insure that the receivers do not get behind them.

This type of defense requires the players to be very disciplined and carry out their assignments. It is effective in long-yardage situations just before the half and at the end of the game to insure a victory.

Coaching is very important to the success of a contain defense. The defensive players must recognize formations, types of running plays, and types of passes and must adjust to stop the play. Figure 8.6 shows a basic alignment of a contain defense.

Defense Team Drills

Name. **Defensive Coverage**

Purpose. To give the defensive backs and linebackers the opportunity to recognize pass routes and cover receivers.

Organization. The skeleton offensive group runs your next opponent's patterns, which the coach has drawn on cards. The quarterback drops to the proper depth and the receivers run the patterns at the appropriate depth of the opponent. The quarterback then throws the ball to the receiver, and the defensive player tries to cover the pattern and intercept the ball (see Figure 8.7). This drill gives the defensive players a chance to work against the pass patterns he'll see in the next game and to work on his execution to stop the pass.

Coaching Points. Emphasize the use of technique and position as dictated by the coverage called. Award a point to the offense for completing a pass and a point to the defense for incomplete or intercepted passes. Play to 10 points.

Name. **Seven on Seven**

Purpose. To allow the defensive line and linebackers to defend the runs that the opponent may use.

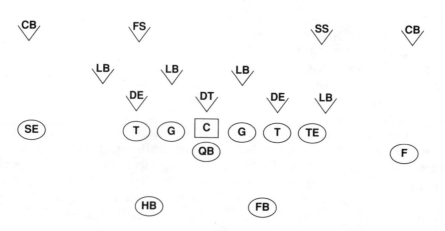

Figure 8.6 Alignment for a contain defense.

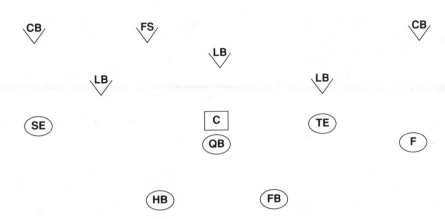

Figure 8.7 Defensive Coverage Drill.

Organization. An offensive team runs the offense from cards showing running plays that the opponent may use in the upcoming game. They block the defense using the same schemes that the opponent will use to give the defense the opportunity to read the blocking, see the backfield action, and react to the plays.

Coaching Points. Watch for proper alignment, individual techniques, and team execution of the called defense.

Special Teams

The special teams play an integral part in football. Special team players need to feel that their contribution to the game is important. You can accomplish this by setting goals for the special teams and by developing a successful strategy.

Goals for Special Teams

The main goal of the special teams is to perform their duties in such a way that they help the team win. You may want to consider some specific goals with your team:

- Know and adhere to the six don'ts:
  - ⊘ Don't be offsides
  - ⊘ Don't rough the kicker
  - ⊘ Don't clip
  - ⊘ Don't block below the waist
  - ⊘ Don't make mistakes
  - ⊘ Don't commit penalties that give the ball back to the offense or give them good field position.
- Win the battle of field position (on a kickoff, keep the opponent inside his

own 30-yard line). This is accomplished by good kicking and good coverage.
- Eliminate bad snaps.
- Make the "big play" (turnovers, blocked kicks, etc.).

Strategies for Special Teams

A simple, basic plan will win the kicking game if it is executed flawlessly and with full effort. The kicking unit's primary objective is to execute the basic elements of the kicking game without making any big mistakes. Its second objective is to attack an opponent's weakness or exploit a situation when it arises.

KICKING GAME RULES

A player signals a fair catch by extending his arm above the head and waving it from side to side. He cannot hit or be hit after a fair catch.

The kicking team may down the football after the ball has hit the ground.

No one on either team can block below the waist.

No player on the receiving team may touch the kicker unless the receiving team has blocked it as the kicker runs with the ball.

A field goal is a scrimmage kick, and the same rules apply as for the punt.

Be alert for a fake punt or field goal attempt at all times.

On a kickoff, after the ball has traveled 10 yards it is a free ball and either team can recover it.

The goal of special teams is to make sure the basics are executed. The punt coverage team must make sure the ball is kicked before they cover. The field goal team must make sure the kick is not blocked before they cover. Also, any time there is a return, the return team must make sure that the other team has actually put the ball in the air to avoid being the victim of a fake play.

By setting goals and developing a sound strategy, you can help make the kicking game a positive part of your football team.

Scrimmages

Scrimmages are simulated game situations. There are different types: full-scale scrimmage, controlled scrimmage, and pass scrimmage.

Full-Scale Scrimmage

The full-scale scrimmage is much like a game situation. Start with a kickoff, punt on fourth down, and keep score. This type of practice activity prepares the offense and defense for competition. However, be cautioned. Any time you use tackling and hitting, you risk injury. If you use the full-scale scrimmage, don't do it on a regular basis.

Controlled Scrimmage

The controlled scrimmage includes some restrictions. The line blocking is live, but the running backs do not get tackled and the quarterbacks and receivers do not get hit. This type of scrimmage helps the team's timing without the risk of injury to key people.

You can use the controlled scrimmage on a regular basis. You may want to emphasize offense for half the scrimmage and defense for the other half. This allows you to use your top players on both offense and defense.

Pass Scrimmage

The pass scrimmage emphasizes passing only. The line is still live in the pass scrimmage, but the quarterback and the receivers are not tackled. The pass scrimmage helps with timing for the passing attack and also gives the defense the opportunity to cover the pass. Use this type of scrimmage on a regular basis because the risk of injury is low and it gives your team a great opportunity to improve its passing attack and pass defense.

Your players can only improve the skills and techniques you teach them if they practice them at full speed in a gamelike situation. For this reason scrimmages are very important in getting your football team ready to play the opponent.

Putting It All Together

Understanding the game, teaching skills, developing a strategy, and formulating a game plan can help make your coaching career successful. However, just because you have taught your players how to block, tackle, and run and pass the football doesn't mean they will always perform these skills successfully in games. Their opponents will have more than a little to say about that.

This *Rookie Coaches Guide* will help you teach the fundamentals of football to your players. And, with the solid foundation you've gained through this book, you should be prepared to move on to teaching your players offensive and defensive football strategies. If you do a good job of teaching, your players will be hooked on football for the rest of their lives. The American Coaching Effectiveness Program has the courses and resources you need to tackle the job.